Unfit for Human Consumption

A Filthy, Poorly Written, One-Handed Book of Poetry

By Gene Rusco

Lubore Publications
Grand Rapids, MI
2024

Contents:

"There is nothing like lechery for putting one in
touch with the beauty in the world."
-Christopher Bram
Lives of Circus Animals

"Tis better to have love and lust
Than to let our apparatus rust."
-Kurt Vonnegut, *God Bless You, Dr. Kevorkian*

"There's looking and there's looking. When some men
look at you it's a greasy thing. It makes you want to
have a bath. With other men it's nice. It helps you
know you're beautiful."
– Patrick Rothfuss, *The Wise Man's Fear*

Apparently publishing companies do not allow outright nudity. Therefore, the nude photos that went along with some of the poetry has been redacted.

[REDACTED]

We at Lubore Publishing are disappointed as some pictures are quite impressive.

<u>Apologies</u>

I offer apologies for what this small book of poetry
entails.

I offer apologies to the people who chose to read
this.

I offer apologies to the people who read poetry for
its grace, thoughtfulness, and elegance
        Of which this book has none.

I offer apologies to the people who are offended by
this book without having read it

I offer apologies to the people who would rather not
read profane words like *cock* or *fuck*
        Of which this book has plenty.

I offer apologies to the people who have read the
Bible and believe it is the word of a god

I offer apologies to the people of all religious faiths
that believe there is a higher being
        For there is none.

I offer apologies to the people I accidentally or
purposely name whether in praise or complaint

I offer apologies to the people named that I no
longer remember

Of which there are plenty named I chose not
to remember.

I offer apologies to people in general
        For we are all fucked.

I am deeply and humbly not sorry for the words
throughout nor the thoughts which went into this

As the Puck says, if we have offended, all is
mended, so goodnight unto you all.

<u>Smooth</u>

My twenties were spent wishing for financial
freedom yet achieved only debt

Spending my weekly pay on books and porn

On knowledge and lust

My thirties were spent whoring when I discovered
the joys of the male anatomy

My forties were spent cleaning up my finances and
STDs

My fifties were spent working, investing, and living
frugally

My sixties were spent being slowly broken down

My seventies were spent realizing that life was
quickly coming to an end

My eighties were spent whoring and blowing my
financial freedom to know that I was not yet dead

My nineties? Who knows other than that I plan to
spend it with smooth twenty-year olds wishing to
achieve financial freedom on their backs.

Perhaps I'll find the perfect boy

One who dotes on me
One who cleans and tidies
One who is intellectual enough
One who enjoys the finer things
One who loves to read
One who I can hold close to at night

But at this point I'll take what I can get.

<u>My Best Friend's Boyfriend's Cock</u>

We have an agreement
My best friend and I

That we share the dicks
We are sent

His boyfriend's dick is tiny
He complains

He sends it to me anyways
Looks good to me

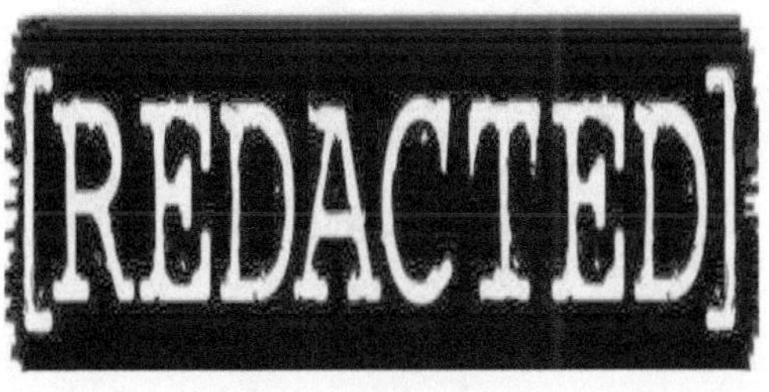

Sadly, the photo that had accompanied this poem
has been redacted. The photo was of a man
wearing boxers loosely in which a flaccid but thick
cock and delectable balls were visible.

<u>Ultimate Wisdom?</u>

If I could back to my younger self knowing I know now

I would be a gym bunny focused on my health with biceps, triceps, and, why the fuck not, quadceps

My ass and abs would be as if chiseled from marble.

I would enjoy attention from other men engaging any and all sexual activities that come my way Including single partners, threesome, fourgies, and orgies…

I would hook up with rich men and live off my looks while pocketing their *goodwill* before moving on

I would enjoy only the best life has to offer.

I would not be meek, thus limiting my chance to inherit, but instead grabbing life by the balls, cock, and tits and giving life a whirl.

Oh, if only I knew then what I know now.

<u>Friends with Benefits</u>

I have been accused of not having friends my own age.

Rather I am only seen out in public with women twice my age

We attend theater, art exhibits, museums, and ballet

We are seen at the best and most exclusive restaurants

But there are of course the boys…
> The Justins, the Ryans, the Taylors/Tylers, and Brents

All of whom lounge around my house indulging in the free alcohol and weed

The Tinas and the Speed.

These emo/jock/goth/nerdy/twink boys love the attention

Corrupting the youth you say?

Well shit, how else would I be able to fuck them?
My winning personality and good looks?

Fuck that!

<u>Hot and Cold</u>

Hot and cold
    Both excuses to get me into bed
    As if it took excuses to get me into bed

Six years apart
    An estranged boyfriend encouraged me to come over one hot summer day
    He was six years older than me
    He had air conditioning. I did not.
    His air conditioning seemed to only work in his bedroom
    We climbed onto his bed where we talked, caught up, and fucked
    I lacked attraction to Steve but sex was sex
    I struggled to get off but eventually came
    I left quickly after and never saw him again

    A guy I don't plan on seeing again
    He was six years younger than me
    He invited me over for dinner one winter's night
    His heating only seemed to work in the bedroom
    After dinner we climbed onto his bed where we talked and then fucked.
    I lacked attraction to this guy whom I can no longer remember his name
    While attempting to get off he tells me about this hunky footballer

With whom he had attended school who
would come over after class
        And fuck his ass
        I quickly came but only because of the
image of the hunky football player

What did these two guys, six years apart, have in
common

Tiny pricks!

Service Announcement:

Be careful with whom you are sexting

They may not be whom they claim

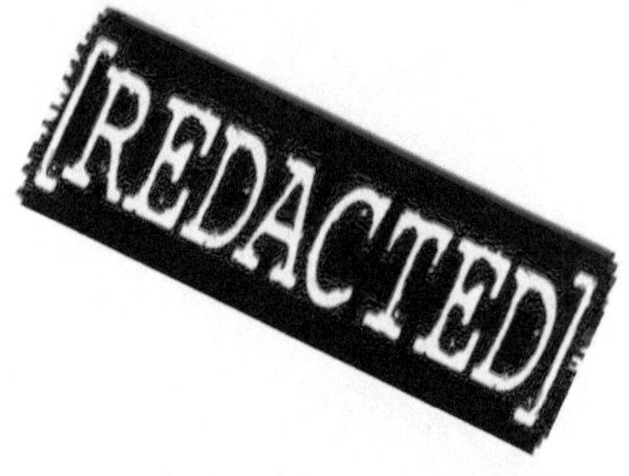

This redaction hurt. A man, taking a selfie of his semi-hard dick, his balls resting on the hem of his pajamas, was beautiful.

The First

My first time with a man was traumatic at the time

He invited me to the bar - I was only 18 but he didn't care

I drank coke and he paid

We closed the bar

He suggested going back to his place

I agreed.

I used his phone to call my mom so she wouldn't worry

Lying that there were a ton of people there.

I used the bathroom, chuckling to myself that he had a purple phone

I walked out   We made out We moved to the bedroom

He strips   I strip

He lays back on the bed and I begin to suck his huge dick

I'm not good but he doesn't seem to notice

Trying to be the best I can I glance up at him for reassurance

His head gently resting on the pillow, his eyes closed

He's passed out

I dress and leave

The next day I walk up to him and ask what needs to be done since after all he was my boss

A decade later and he still had no memory of that night

Earning Cock

Justin's cock

So long

So Beautiful

Pointing to Heaven

I can't stop picturing it

But maybe…

When I'm thin enough
When I'm rich enough
When I'm cool enough
When I'm smart enough
When I'm muscular enough
When I'm worthy enough

Maybe…

He'll let me jerk it
He'll let me suck it
He'll fuck me
He'll fill me up with cum

But maybe…

When I'm enough I won't need him.

The God Ryan

There have been many Ryan's in my life.

> Brother-in-law
> Coworkers
> Employees
> Friends

There was one such friend of a friend with whom
was the God Ryan

After a heavy night of drinking
He arose from my couch like a phoenix

His usual emo unassumingness
His usual dark baggy clothes
Were gone

He wore only boxers

Revealing gleaming hard flesh
His muscular arms
His abs
His thick thighs
His smooth body

Only his cock was hidden from my view

He would have been the envy of the Greek gods

This the God Ryan

<u>Dream #1</u>

I had a dream the other night

Perhaps I saw something I shouldn't have

Perhaps I read something I shouldn't have

It made me laugh later when I recalled it

I had a dream in which I was getting a blow job
from a hot woman

Then I peed on her.

I had a dream the other night.

Who knows where such dreams come from

<u>Lust</u>

When working at a library I had some
young studs working for me

The problem was that I kept getting them confused
Although if they would have gone to bed with me

I am sure I would have remembered them by face

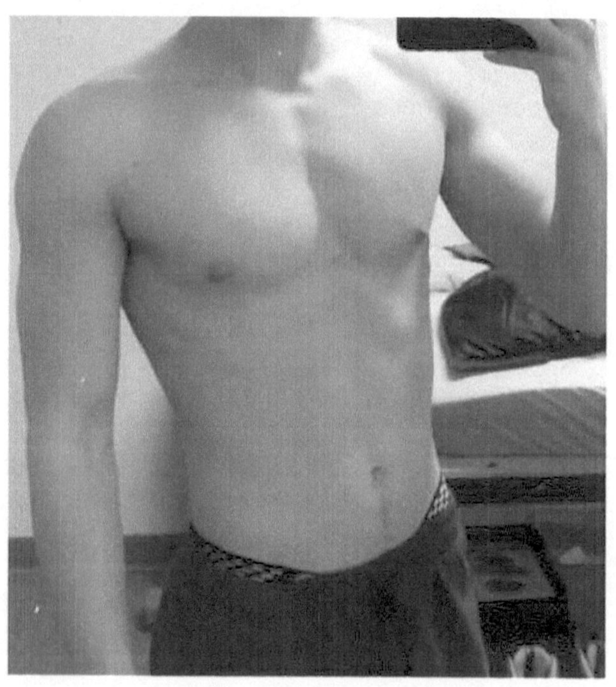

<u>The Boy</u>

His walk   So brilliant
His pace   So oblivious to time

He wears his hair long like an emo
He wears loose baggy clothing

Yet other times he wears almost nothing at all
On the hottest of days he strolls around the
neighborhood in nothing but loose shorts
On these days his short stature is all on display
        His muscular arms
        His flat muscular stomach
        His smooth body

I've talked to him only once
        He spoke so assuredly
        No sign of hesitation
        No sign of embarrassment

He asked me how much his time was worth to me

I thought to myself the world!

Though I knew he were only joking

And so I said I'll pass

A sentence I have regretted everyday since even
though the boy with whom I desired was only
sixteen

Booty Call

The 20-year-old former lover called
I was working so he left a message
That he wanted to come over

I called him back inviting him over
It had been a dry spell

We grabbed dinner
Went back to my house
Where we listened to music
He hates classical... Loves country
I hate country... Loves classical

Bored with conversation
What did we have in common
That had kept us together

We cuddle
Start making out
Pawing one another

I reached into his pants
Grabbed his four-inch cock
Giving it a few tugs
Sucking on his ear lobe

He starts jerking my dick
Through my slacks
Refusing to kiss me

I try to get his pants off
He goes limp
Excuses himself
Not into it anymore

He leaves within minutes

I wasted four hours on a failed booty call

When I was in seventh grade a classmate drew a
penis and balls to look like a tower.

He supposedly hid the drawing behind a picture in
the classroom.

I looked for days trying to find it.

When guys send me pics like this it makes me think
of that drawing.

And perhaps if I climb enough mountains I will
reach the heavens.

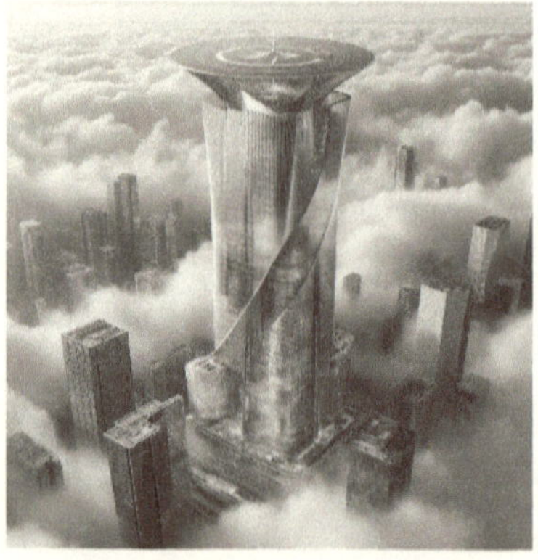

The original photo that went along with this poem
has been reacted. So, I found an image of a tower
with two small buildings attached. The original
photo was much more impressive with a long, hard
cock pointing to the heavens.

The reason for my low self-worth
Is that people can so easily
Cancel plans with me

They don't care how it makes me feel

Only how it affects them

They cancel
They move
They leave

And I am alone

Sent:

Thursday, January 15, 2009
4:57pm

<u>Dream #2</u>

I had a dream the other night

Perhaps I saw something I shouldn't have

Perhaps I read something I shouldn't have

I had a dream in which President Clinton was being chased by a Rancor

I had a dream the other night.

Fucking weird

<u>Visitation</u>

Standing line to see a dead man

Listening to old men talk of tractors, farming, and batteries

How dull are conversations I am not a part of

Standing in line in an opulent church

Hating how long this is taking
Hating people who don't know line etiquette
Hating people who talk incessantly

Staring at cute mournful boys gets boring after awhile

I hope I only have to do this once a year

I hope I only have to be in a church once a year

Wondering where everyone I know is

Bored–Dull–Uninteresting–Dull–Bored

Looking at pictures of the dead man enjoying life
                How ironic

I hope my visitation will be more interesting

But knowing who will plan it… I doubt it.

<u>Stolen Poem</u>

This is a poem that was inserted into this book by a former friend with whom the author had hoped to fuck. The friend was obstinately straight which blue balled the author no matter how much booze and weed was provided.

I've succumbed to a sickness…
Unfortunately.

Yes, it is quite unfortunate
That I am
Dying

Doctor told me
"It's terminal"

"Well Shit," I said.

"Shit indeed," replied the doc.

I asked if there was anything I could do.

"Pray," said doc.

I then realized
I was fucked

I went home
Laid down on my bed
Masturbated

Had a cigarette

Fucked I remained.

Author note: He may have remained fucked but not by Gene Rusco even after I allowed him to write in my journal.

Whatever, I'm still not bitter after a couple of decades apart. Move on. Get over it.

The poem by Taylor may be the best poem in this book hence why I stole it. Hope you enjoyed it. Maybe bookmark it so you can come back from time to time for a reprieve.

<u>Ex-Boyfriend</u>

A boyfriend and I once discussed our favorite
moments of porn

He loved to watch cum shots. To see the man
climax.

I loved the lead up to the climax. The second
before he cums.

I loved the suspense, the drama, the anticipation
He was all for instant gratification.

A long, leaky dick was
originally here but had to be
redacted due to the puritanical
laws and "morals" of this
country. Trust me when I say
that the photo fit the poem
perfectly.

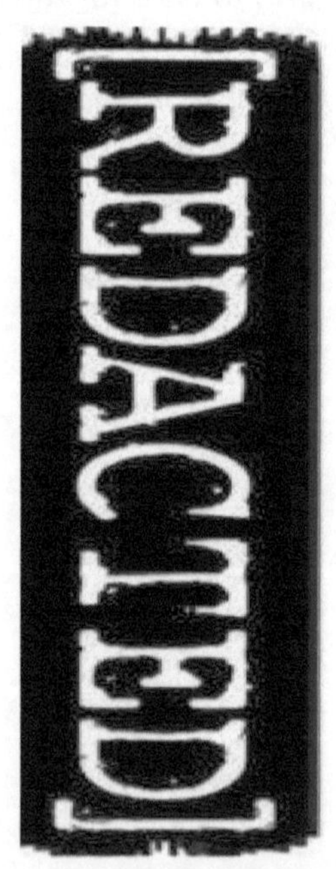

<u>Experimentation</u>

I always suspected I was a bottom.

Always eager to please with my customer service
attitude

"How may I help you?"
"Would you like fries with that?"
"Paper or plastic?"
"Will that be all tonight?"
"Is there anything else I can do for you?"

Not having a chance to get a real dick up my ass
I experimented.

Dildos, cucumbers, celery, hotdogs; both frozen
and thawed, as well as other phallic objects

All leaving me limp, unsatisfied, and often soggy

So one night
Watching porn at two
With the help of lube
I put a finger up my ass

Then two

Then three

I came… Hard… As if I were a twelve year old boy
jizzing for the first time!

<u>Celestial Thunder</u>

An aphrodisiac enjoyed by the Yin Dynasty king,
Chou-Hsin (1154-1122 BCE) as stated by the *Tales
from Early Histories* written by Chinese historian
Ssu-Ma.

It consists of
     -Tongues of a hundred peacocks
     -Spiced with chili powder
     -Flavored with the sperm of pubescent boys

I don't know about you but the peacocks can keep
their tongues and the sperm…

Well, I prefer that straight from the hose.

<u>Kimber</u>

My assistant, my friend, my enforcer, my drinking
companion

She said there were too many Kims and Kimberlys
in the world

She threatened people who looked at us wrong

She shook her tits at old guys

She drank too fast. She got drunk too fast

She was 40 with two boys; an 18 year old sailor
and a 14 year-old she hadn't seen in a few years

She died June 25, 2008 in a drunk driving accident

She the passenger, the driver drunk
Her friend lived

People say Kimber died to give us an example of
what could happen

I think that's bullshit

The service was unorganized
The pastor an ass who never met her

And so after the funeral we went to a bar and
toasted Kimber

<u>Faith</u>

Paternal grandparents were church going Christian
Reformed and the biggest hypocrites and terrible
people

Maternal grandparents were nonchurch going
Catholics and the kindest, warmest people

My father is a churchgoing Reborn Christian
And the worst money grubbing, starfucking,
adulterer

My mother is a nonchurch going Catholic
Who loves and tries not to judge

My brother is a Baptist minister who believes in
love, only when it relates to male-female
relationships

My sister is a church going nondenominational
Christian who's husband refused to attend our gay
wedding but felt shunned by his family when they
became Catholics and none in his family approved

Me? A Douglas Adams' Atheist, who once said that
he avoids calling himself an agnostic as it gives
those of faith to believe that he at least had some
faith in a higher power.

Faith: "Belief that does not rest on logical proof or
material evidence. Amen to that!

<u>Dearest Ryan</u>
(reflection of the lost Ryan)

There once was a boy named Ryan.

We started working together at 16. I was a few months older.

We hung out at work and enjoyed conversing.

He played the clarinet and I played the trumpet in band but we went to different schools.

I moved to a different department when he moved from bagboy to cashier.

I came back to the department and we worked closely together.

He went off to college whereas I continued working.

He would come back during school breaks and holidays.

We started getting closer. Only when we were 21 did we each learn the other was gay.

He made me dinner. He came as my date to a family wedding.

We spoke for hours on the phone.

We went clothes shopping, out to restaurants, and even to the theater.

I loved him but was too unsure of myself to know if we were dating.

Then one day when I called to see if he wanted to hang out did I learn that he moved to another state and I would never talk or see him again.

Twenty years later and I wonder if he ever thinks of me as I think of him.

<u>The Boone to my Bane</u>
(original poem about the lost Ryan)

The Love of my life

Looking back on our past

We worked together from bagboys to management

We went to dinners
We came out together
We went to clubs and danced

We saw La Cage Falles
        Where his brother played a drag queen

We saw movies
We went shopping together
He made me dinner

He went to my cousin's wedding
We talked on the phone for hours
        Until they died

In my mind we date
In my mind he was perfect
In my mind we were perfect

He was funny, intelligent, and attractive.

Gawd, how I miss him.

<u>The Waiter</u>

I used to go to this restaurant the same day at the
same time every week

The waiter was a sweet young man who always
remembered my order.

If only I could have ordered him to go!

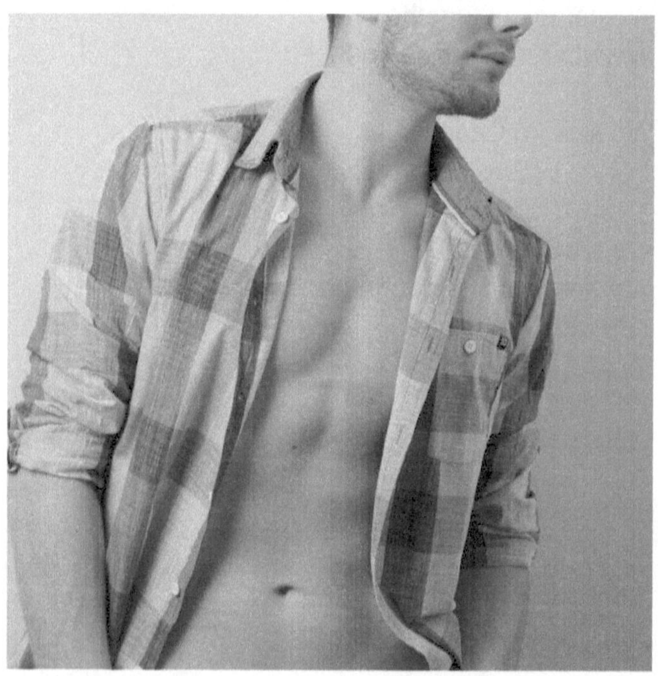

Almost a Race Riot

A. "What specifically did you call her?"
Q. " I called her a fucking bitch."

A. "Do you have anger or racial issues?"
Q. "No. Just calling a spade a spade."

A. "You do not take pills or have taken anger management classes?"
Q. "No. I was upset after she verbally abused me for over ten minutes."

A. "You were angry and called a customer a fucking bitch?"
Q. "Yes, of course looking back there were many different ways this could have been handled better but at the time I was angry."

A. "You called an African American woman a fucking bitch in front of a large group of African American customers and about started a race riot as they started to try and beat down the office door to drag you out?"
Q. "Apparently."

A. "You know there is no way for us to proceed without letting you go?"
Q. "Yes."

<u>Weak Will</u>

I have always been weak-willed

The subservient friend

The ever pleasing bottom

Easy prey for peer pressure

Always doing what I ought not to do

Always on a diet but always breaking it within hours
if not minutes

After ordering a pizza and forcing myself to only eat
half rather than the whole pie

Like some gluttonous slug

A night of sleeplessness and grease induced
nightmares

I decided it best to toss the rest but as I stood there
over the trash

Contemplating eating the remaining pizza

But managed to slide them off the plate.

Yet still there remained a lone bacon bit

Clinging to hold on…

So tempted was I that I took that piece of bacon
and about ate it

But managed to throw it in the trash anyways
against all my inner demons screaming to eat it

Perhaps I am stronger than I thought.

<u>Dream #4</u>
(I am skipping the poem about
dream #3 as it was lame. Something
to do with being Captain America
and hunting zombies)

I had a dream last night

It involved a sexy employee of mine

A dark-skinned white boy with beautiful brown eyes

And a naive looking mouth that looked like it wanted to kiss

His body is slight and boyish

I have often daydreamed about having his lips around my
cock

But this dream was different

It was nonsexual

Instead we sat on my couch and smoked pot.

How odd... is that?

<u>The Owner's Son</u>

Sam…

The owner's son

Geeky

Pudgy

Unsure

Unsteady

Absolutely adorable

Alone in my office he says he has a question for me

An odd question

A tough question

Yes, yes yes!! I thought to myself, I would love to have dinner, love to date, love you

But as he stood there without saying a word

Then said he couldn't remember what he was going to ask.

Damn!

<u>Hoops</u>

One advantage of working near a park is the joy of seeing a fit young man shooting hoops.

This young man came by almost everyday that summer and sweated down his perfect chest and abs.

Unfortunately my phone camera lacked the telescopic lens I needed to get better shots of this perfect specimen of manhood.

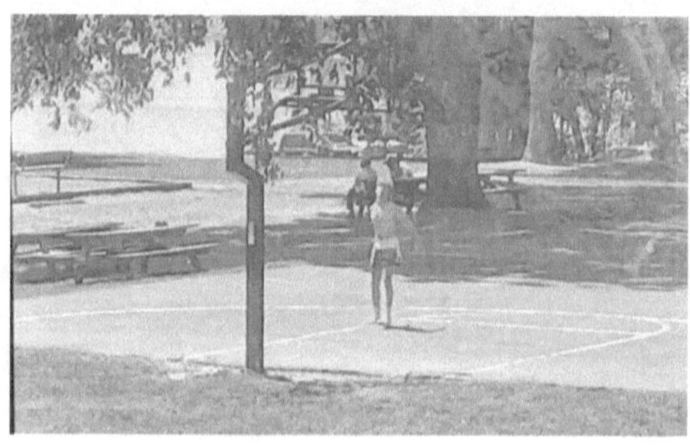

<u>Books</u>

Here I sit in my Queen Anne chair chain smoking
my Camel Number Nines
        The ones with the pink camel on the pack

Reading a flurry of my favorite queer authors;
        Edmund White, Christopher Bram, Stan
Leventhal, and Felice Picano

Reading a flurry of my favorite straight-ish authors
        Shakespeare sonnets, Doyle's Sherlock,
Christie's Poirot, and Stout's Wolfe

Listening to an array of music;
        Mozart, Dido, Beethoven, Cher, and Techno

Daydreaming of the men in my life;
Their dicks, their cocks, and the sucking and
fucking or the lack thereof

As they're almost all straight
As they're almost all taken

Some gay enough to lead me on
But not gay enough to follow through

Dirty old man that I am continue to lust and flirt
Until I am eighty and find myself sitting in my
Queen Anne chair surrounded by my loving, filthy
books

<u>Joe and Taylor</u>

<u>Or</u>

<u>Taylor and Joe</u>

The oddest pairing I know.
Is Joe and Taylor… or Taylor and Joe

One a pacifist… the other not Taylor and Joe

One hardworking… the other not Joe and Taylor

One who spends time on appearances… the other
not   Taylor and Joe

One jock and one emo Joe and Taylor

They have their fights
        But soon make up

So much alike
        Yet so different

These two heterosexual (???) boys complete one
another

Hurt when plans are made without the other

How beautiful and odd are Taylor and Joe… or Joe
and Taylor

A Perfect Diversion

Having attended a group outing with coworkers at a
hockey game
Hosted by a large alcohol producing and
distributing company
With free food and free booze

I tottered down the street back to my car,
conveniently parked in front of my favorite bar
Drinking a glass of $5 chardonnay I looked around
and found myself surrounded by old men
I quickly left and walked to the closest club full of
beautiful boys

I had my eye on a guy
Whom I saw as a long-term prospect
Building my courage one drink at a time

When a young 19-year-old hung on my arm
Kevin was small, young, hot, firm, and utterly
perfect
Sociable, built, and an incredible ass

He held onto me as I held onto him
I was the envy of the bar
Standing center stage with the catch of the day

He kept saying he had a wealthy, older boyfriend
who would be back any time
Yet as the night progressed none appeared.

The night came to an end and having to get up
early
I made for the door without Kevin
And even worse without a phone number

<u>Cricket</u>

While waiting for my pizza I sat in my car outside a
strip mall of crappy stores.

Through the window I could view this hot young guy

At the Cricket store!

Oh, how I longed to inquire about other tattoos
hidden from view.

And how I wanted us to rub our legs together to
make beautiful music

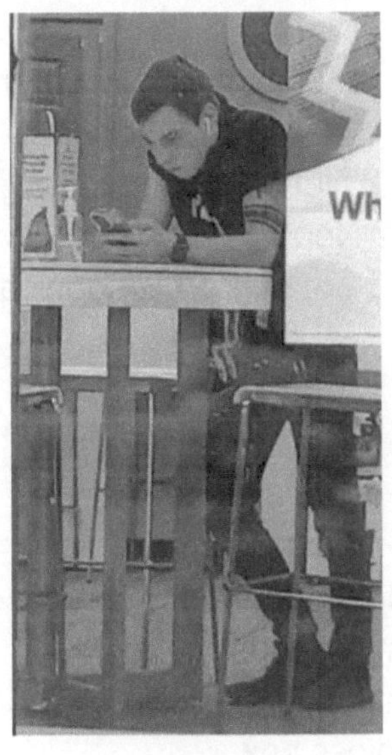

<u>Me?</u>

Being single

I have lots of time to focus on the most important thing in my life…

ME!!!

Age? 20s when I started this, 40s when publishing this
Gay? Yup
Work? Customer service for 20 years and library work for the past 5 years
Politics? Socialist liberal but realistic when it comes to voting
Culture? Love reading, music, theater, and musicals
People person? Not so much
Technological? Nope.
Religion? None-not nun. Philosophically atheist.

I need to flee-

Flee from self-complacence
Flee from self-indulgence
Flee from straight suburbia
Flee from boring friends
Flee from exhausting exes
Flee from mindless sex
Flee from meaningless and low paying jobs
Flee from always being agreeable

<u>Black Beauty</u>

While intoxicated at a wine tasting in a suave hotel
in Kalamazoo

I was watching the fishes swimming in the giant
aquarium

When I noticed that on the other side of the
aquarium was the hotel pool
Full of bloated, hairy old men with their screaming
annoying children
And wives yelling from their poolside deck chairs to
be careful

But then I saw
Under the faux rocky waterfall
Was the most beautiful teenage black boy
No older than 19

Under the cascading waterfall
Water streaming down his beautiful body
Clad in only a tight pair of swim shorts

As I watched from the safety from the other side of
the aquarium
He swam, played, dived, and splashed
I watched his muscles, his abs, his chest, his arms,
his legs move and thicken
It caused my cock to move and thicken!

It is one of the most wondrous sights on Earth to
see

A black beauty.

<u>Internet Porn</u>

I was accused of viewing Internet porn on the work
computers

My boss called me and told me that I need to come
clean
            That I need to confess all
                    His computer was full of viruses from
Internet porn

Later he told me to forget it
            That there was a new policy on Internet
usage
                    Specifically about Internet porn

When I spoke with Human Resources
            They told me that the entire computer had
to be disposed of
                    There were just too many viruses

When I asked about the Internet porn
            I was told the computer had almost been
exclusively used
                    To view Internet porn
                            And that the porn was naked
women

I was innocent of looking at Internet porn

My boss on the other hand had a lot to explain!

<u>Faith</u>

I was raised in the Christian Reformed Church
Where everyone seemed phony to me
With their coffee and tea
Asking how are you today but not waiting or caring
about the answer.
So quick to spread gossip like manure

All of Christianity seemed one big hoax. So I quit
Christianity.
      Judaism is just pre-Christianity and Islam is
post Christianity.

Buddhism is too hard with always thinking
positively. I am too cynical for that.
      Other Eastern religions seem too much like
mythology to me
      If I wanted myths I could go for Egyptian or
Norse.
      Greek is too soap opera for me and Roman
myths are just Greek-Lite

I had missionaries from the Church of the Latter-
Day Saints visit
      Three cute boys coming to my house to
discuss their beliefs
      It was adorable watching them
      Tell me about Jesus visiting the Native
Americans
      And that Heaven is a planet that orbits the
sun exactly opposite of Earth

And John Smith found gold plates in his
backyard that only he could read
    Because an angel gave him special
glasses...which he lost several times
    Sadly it all fell apart when an old grizzled
deacon of the church
    Came to say these special in-home visits
were coming to an end
    And no more cute boys could visit me

Agnosticism is too much work- there is something,
there is nothing

Atheism- the belief in nothing... A true dichotomy

I haven't a clue and that's my faith... or the lack
thereof.

<u>Mom Pants</u>

I worked with this cute young guy

He was smart and articulate and kind

His smile was infectious and made him oh so
attractive

Yet on this day he decided to wear mom pants that
rode up his ass and was not hot at all.

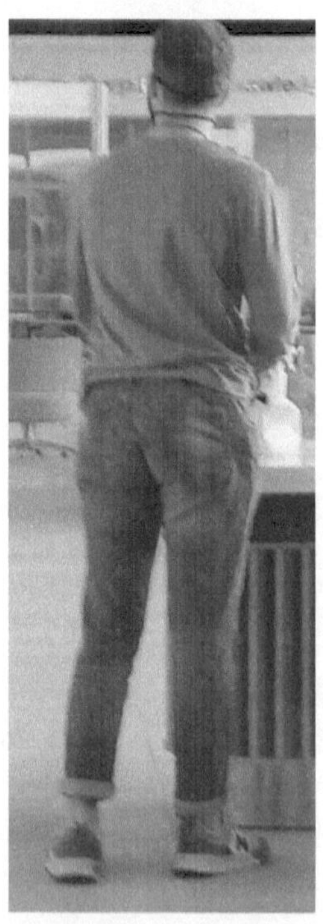

<u>August 15, 2009</u>

Our second date, dinner at five, at the Grand
Rapids Brewing Company
Long before it was actually located in downtown
Grand Rapids
Long before it had downtown prices

He had Pinot Grigio and I had Riesling
It takes us half an hour to realize that we hadn't
even looked at the menu
We each order a burger with bacon; mine with
cheddar and his with gouda

We talk of the British sitcoms we love
We talk of the musicals, the theater, and the
Shakespeare we love
We talk of towns and locations we love
We talk of all the hobbies we have in common

We go to Barnes and Noble and shop the dollar
tables
We sit in his car and talk for hours

We part at nine, unwillingly

RIP James

<u>Annoyances of a College Classroom</u>

Tap tap tap of the laptop keys
Tap tap tap of the laptop keys
Crinkle crinkle crinkle of the Subway wrapper
Crunch crunch crunch of the potato chips

Tap tap tap of the laptop keys
Tap tap tap of the laptop keys
Slurp slurp slurp of the fountain pop
Gulp gulp gulp of the 20oz pop

Tap tap tap of the laptop keys
Tap tap tap of the laptop keys
Um, er, uhs of the students
Um, er, uh of the professors

Tap tap tap of the laptop keys
Tap tap tap of the laptop keys
Crinkle crinkle crinkle of the candy bar wrapper
Click, slam, click of the classroom door

Tap tap tap of the laptop keys
Tap tap tap of the laptop keys

How does anyone get anything done

Fragile emperor going going home

Downtown, it fled home

Fly fly fly

Spy spy spy

The God Delusion

Most able son, not oldest

So what?

The Fountain of Youth

Unlike most people
I have discovered the fountain of youth

I lived near it throughout my twenties
It was always there
I assumed it always would be

I figured I would drink of it when I was older
Old enough to feel I needed it

I always envisioned myself drinking from it
The sweet taste on my lips and tongue
The warm fluid gushing down my throat
Coating the stomach lining with its deliciousness

Many nights I dreamed of drinking from the fountain
of youth
Believing it would be there in the morning

Oh how I looked forward to the day
That I would drink its refreshing liquid

Yet one day
I looked upon it and found it empty

<u>Nudes? Where?</u>

This hot young guy whom I met online

Informed the world that he could never be president
due to the amount of nudes of him online

Trust me when I say that they are not easy to find
As I found none!

What a tease!

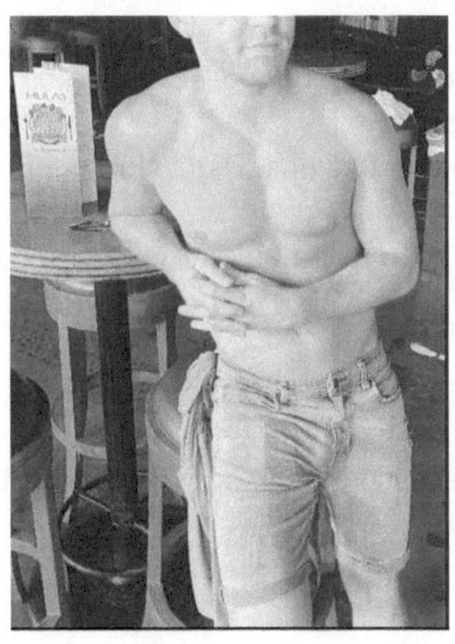

<u>The Right One</u>

Do we focus too much on the Right One?

How can we ever know who is the Right One?

Life is like a bar-
        Always looking to the door for the new
arrival
        Judging them as they come in
        Are they better than being alone
        Are they better than the one I'm with

Isn't saying "I've found the Right One"
        Just saying
"I've settled for this one, Right Now" ???

We are expected to meet, fall in love and marry the
Right One

To dedicate ourselves to the Right One

But I keep looking to the door for the Next One

<u>Gibberish</u>

Love, Fly Away
          Be sure Labor Union
Love, this is my song

20 19 18 17 16 15

Positive, Negative
          Downtown
Sweet Love
          Whatever
Stalin & Aristotle

14 13 12 11 10 9

Cause they
          Don't know
About us
          Diogenes
His Banner
          Over me
                    Is Love
Refresh me
          With

8 7 6 5 4 3

Apples
          Arms race breeds distrust

2 1

<u>Cincerous</u>

Crazy drive on my ass

Moved over to allow her to pass

As soon as she got by
        She slowed down

I moved back behind her
        Where she fluctuated between 60 and 80

A truck almost slammed into me
        As she braked for no apparent reason

This driver had Cincerous on her back window
        I think its Spanish for Fucking Crazy Bitch

I got by her as she turned into a bagel shop

She had a little girl in the backseat

Great! I thought, she's training a future Cincerous.

Libertarian Self-Delusional Letter to the Government

Dear Government,

Stay out of my car
    I like to text

Stay off my roads
    I like to speed

Stay out of my front seat
    I refuse to wear a seatbelt

Stay out of my bar
    I like to smoke indoors

Stay out of my bedroom
    I like to have sex

Stay out of my house
    I like to own a gun

Stay out of my space
    I like to smoke weed

Stay out of my head
    I like to think what I want to think

Stay out of my school
    I like to learn what I want to learn

Stay out of my library
       I like to read what I want to read

Stay out of mouth
       I like to curse

Stay out of my life
       I'm fine without you

At least for now

Why, oh why, am I such a sucker for a dumb faced boy?

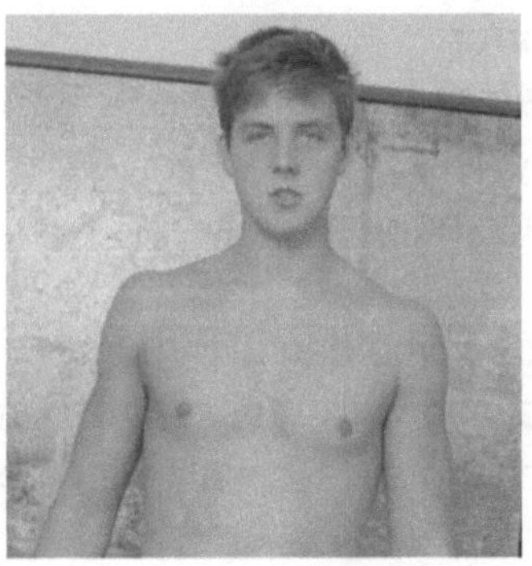

Thanks to Corbin Fisher @ corbinfisher.com for the permission to use this picture of "Caden"

Corbin Fisher also gave permission to use several other pictures but even after censuring them slightly, the publishing company asked that they be completely removed. I find this boy and his body to be absolutely stunning.

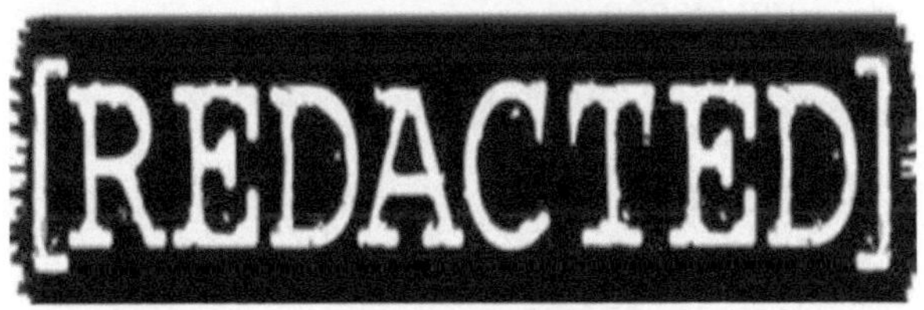

<u>Sweet Story</u>

All life is a story

It may be a fairy tale
      Or horror
      Or literary
      Or mystery
      Or a mixed genre

There are those who dance through
      Some who walk against the herd
      Some who always walk with the crowd

Each event a new chapter in our life
      Birth
      Baby to child
      Child to teen
      Teen to adult
      Adult to Old Age
      Death

Life Moments
      First kisses
      First fuck
      Marriage
      Divorce
      Children
      Parents' deaths
      Spousal death
      Child death
      Retirement

Comfortable living
Worrisome Instances
Hurtful Choices
Some experience some, some more than others

But ultimately like all stories they end.

Don't delude yourself
There is no epilogue, no sequel, no afterlife

We end. Our story forgotten. A book placed on the
shelf to collect dust after we become dust.

<u>Road Head</u>

I have a second cousin who was giving her boyfriend road head and at the point of climax he jerked off the road and hit a tree

He was killed instantly

Punned Distracted Driving Kills

Based on the image you can see dick, poking out pair of jeans was angle. The was taken sitting in seat of The and

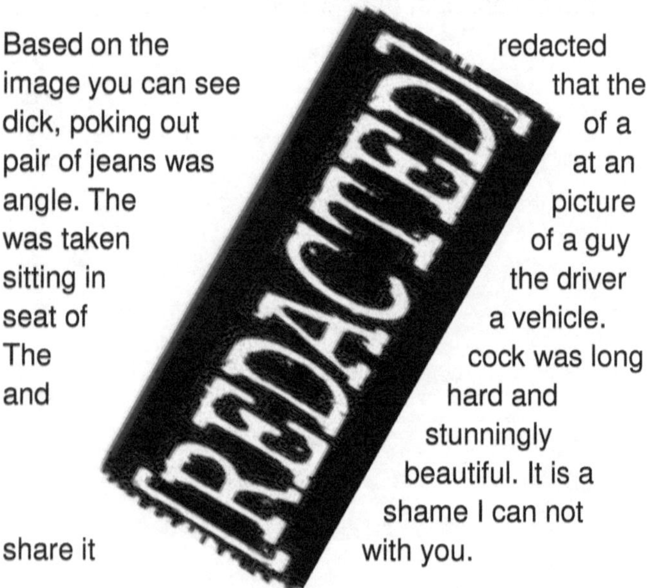

redacted that the of a at an picture of a guy the driver a vehicle. cock was long hard and stunningly beautiful. It is a shame I can not

share it with you.

<u>Politicians</u>

Who would you rather have for president?

An elitist or the guy next door?

An elitist being someone who understands;
        Economics
        Foriegn relations
        Tariffs
        Taxes
        Immigration
        Technology
        Science
        Global Warming
        Space Travel
        Historical Effects on Present Events
        Religious Differences
        Cultural Differences

Versus…

The guy next door
        That you can discuss fantasy football with
        That you can have a beer with
        That you can shoot the shit with
        That you understand 100% of the time

I think I prefer the days when leaders were
intellectual elites rather than some asshole born
with a silver spoon in their mouth pretending to be
the guy next door.

<u>Dream #5</u>

I had a dream last

I have no idea where such dreams come from

Perhaps too many drag shows?

Perhaps too much time with family?

I had a dream

That I was with my grandmother
I was wearing drag
Made from her clothes
That she crocheted.

She thought I looked lovely.

I had a dream last night.

It was freaky.

<u>Dream #6</u>

I had a dream last night

Normally I go on and on about where dreams come from
        but tonight I want to focus on the dream

I dreamed of my first love
I dreamed we were together
The dream was so vivid
        I can remember his look
        His smell
        His essence.

I dreamed too much.
        I remembered his argumentativeness
        His questioning
        His intelligence

I ended up leaving him for my current love.

Could it be that I have grown?
        That I have moved on?

I certainly hope so.

I had a dream last night.

<u>Three Boys</u>

Authors note. This page has remained blank for years. It was partially based on a dream I had but also about some employees or friends of mine. I am unsure which combination of three boys it was going to be about.

I do remember it was going to be a menage a troi but again I can't remember who the boys were.

I can say that I have almost been in three menage a trois. The first was when I was in my early twenties and my boss and I were at the bar when he hooked up with a guy in an alleyway. They wanted to go back to the other guy's house but I was driving. They asked if I wanted to participate but I was too much of a prude at that point in my life. The second potential menage a trois was with a 19 year old boy and my female best friend. The boy and I were all for it but she was not. The third potential menage a trois was with an employee of mine who was in his early twenties and a chick at a party. We were doing a "If you show me yours I'll show you mine" when I backed out and went home. More about this is in the next poem.

Sorry for the long story about my lack of threesomes and explanation as to why this title lacked a poem to go along with it.

<u>Lament</u>

Almost ten years ago (even more now)
A boy of twenty flirted with me
He was such a beautiful boy.

We worked together
We partied together
We hung out together

He offered me a threesome
        With him and a girl
        He knew of my infatuation
He was too straight to have sex without a girl

I took him up on his offer
He pulled out his dick in front of me and the girl
It was flaccid but it was beautiful
But when it came time for me to show mine
I chickened out.

I saw him recently with his new girlfriend
He put on a few pounds
He lost some hair
He lost his boyish looks

But he is still so beautiful

<u>Boring</u>

Hot EMT taking a sexy pic in the bathroom mirror…

Perhaps if he were showing a nipple I wouldn't be so weirded out by the toilet behind him

Kinda upset not to see a dick poking through the folds of the shirt

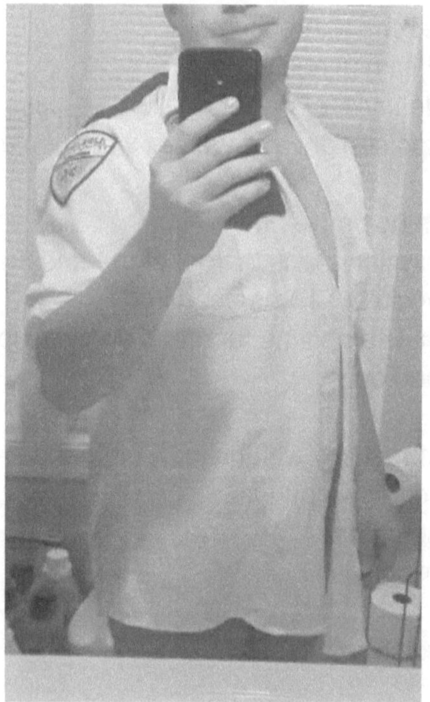

Side note: Good thing there is no dick present as I would have had to redact this picture too.

<u>Contemplating Lunch</u>

I was talking with a friend of mine when we started to discuss Art Films

"I hate artsy, fartsy, low budget films," I said. "I hate them because they show a woman's tits every five minutes but never show a man's balls."

"Balls are gross," she replied.

"Balls, like peanut butter bacon cheeseburgers, are delicious."

"You're disgusting! Balls don't taste like your lunch!"

"That depends," I replied, "if you smear peanut butter, bacon, ketchup, and mustard on them and cover it all with cheese followed by a thorough licking, then they would. Great! Now I'm hungry and horny!"

"That's fucking nasty, you nasty fuck!" she retorted.

"Yeah it really is. You could get really sick licking raw bacon grease off some guy's scrotum."

"Now I'm going to vomit," she commented as she quickly left the room.

Gene's Hollywood Kiss

You know that scene at the end of classic movies where there's a kiss and the couple part ways never to see each other again? It is the most bittersweet of large screen moments. This is my Hollywood Screen Kiss.

He called to say he was moving to Chicago in the morning. This would be my last chance to hang out with him.

He and a group of friends were chilling in a gay bar, even though they were all straight. I rushed downtown to see him. We hung out wandering from bar to bar until the bars closed and we were being forced to part.

We walked back to my friend's car that late evening. Unsure when we would see each other again we said goodbye for the hundredth time.

My friend yelled "Just kiss him already!"

He grabbed my coat and pulled me for a kiss. It was sweet. It was gentle. It was perfect. We hugged and said our last goodbye.

He turned and walked away. I climbed into my friend's car and watched as he walked down the street away from me. At the end of the block he turned and disappeared from view.

<u>Chance Encounters</u>

I have had sex with 16 individuals.

The first time I had sex was with a girl in high school when I was pretending to be bisexual. We dated for a little bit but she was always eager to make out. On Thanksgiving we were in my room, she was naked, and I was going down on her. I think that's when she realized I was faking being interested in girls.

The next person I had sex with was my boss. You can read about that failed sexual experience in the poem "The First." He attempted to have sex with me more after I moved into his spare bedroom but I refused.

The third person I had sex with was a guy that I hung out with that I worked with but not actually dating. It was a year from the time we last saw each other to reconnecting for a one-time hookup. It was utterly devastating.

The fourth person was a beautiful Puerto Rican. We connected on Craigslist. I learned that if I said I was bisexual and my girlfriend was okay with me sleeping with guys it got me a lot more attention. I went over to his house between college classes and sucked him off. His dick was almost taller than he was! He is also the only hookup that I never learned his name.

Then came the bathroom hookups. One guy would meet me in the basement bathroom of the community college, fuck my face, cum down my throat, and be gone. We did that twice. He had a tiny cock but was a nice guy.

Then I started dating a much older man. He was a sweet guy, wealthy, and considerate. He lived in the Flint area and would drive two hours or more to pick me up or to meet me for dinner. He was heavy and once we were taking a soak in his hot tub we got stuck. It required heaving myself out of the tub to get us unstuck. But when I found out that both his children were older than me it was over.

So, what do I do when I find the guy I'm dating is 30+ years older than me? Date someone ten years younger than myself! It was actually closer to six but you get the point. We dated but one night I called and he had company and if he could call back. Turned out that his high school fuck friends were still his fuck friends who would drop by on occasion. I didn't mind too much as long as he told me but when I started lusting after his stories more than him it made me realize there was no future for us.

The eighth was a guy who stayed with my cousin. He was a trashy, unibrowed, hairy, twenty-year old. He had the sweetest smile and radiated charm. He also had the look of needing to be cared for. He also had a huge dick that I loved to suck. Until he started sleeping with another cousin of mine. I most certainly did not want to touch anything she had with a ten-foot pole.

The ninth guy was my cousin's husband. He was an actual bisexual who had never had sex with a guy before. So, one night when their kids were out of the house he attempted to fuck me with his teeny dick, got off in the condom, rolled over, and fell asleep with his wife. I went back to the couch.

I'm not sure if I should count D2. We flirted. He claimed to be bisexual. He had some traumatic sexual issues so sex for him was iffy. We were watching a show and I started to rub him through his sweatpants. Then I went under the sweatpants... but he never got hard and I got bored. So, sex 9.5?

The tenth guy was someone else I hooked up with on Craigslist where I pretended to be a bisexual with a girlfriend. This guy was also in the grocery world and we hooked up a lot. Always at his house at random times of the day. Once he had family staying with him so we met up in his storage unit. This is also the first time I tried poppers and they gave me a headache.

The eleventh is my husband with whom I have been faithful for the last 10 years. My husband is also the only guy to fuck me fully.

I am sure there are others but the memory of them and of the sex act is long gone.

Like the sex with people I can't remember this dick is unknown to me. Someone sent it to me but the who is lost to time.

Redacted because of a hard cock in the picture. Shame because it was quite nice even if I don't remember who it belonged too. It was another tower shot of a penis. Straight up and pointing to the heavens.

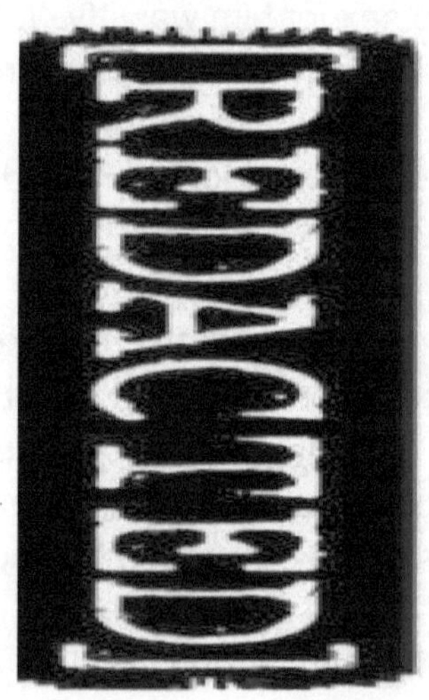

The End

I started writing this book of "poetry" in my early twenties. The last "poem" was written when I was 26 or 27. The handwritten book of poems was tossed into a desk drawer and rarely moved.

So why publish this book of bad poetry? First off, this is the creme de la creme of the poems. There are over 60 handwritten poems but those that I did cut were extremely lame. Often having to do with books, me, or family in a self-effacing way that looking back on them feels embarrassing. Yes, I know there's other self-effacing poems throughout that are embarrassing so you can understand that if I did cut one, there was a really good reason.

But back to why I decided to publish.

I was at a book fair in Ann Arbor, MI and saw a book entitled *Live Nude Guys*. It is a short book of poetry. The title and cover drew me in. I talked to the publisher representing the book. He informed me that they only publish books that hold a certain charm or talent. They only publish one or two books per year based on their criteria and discriminant preferences.

The book is less than 40 pages. It is mostly about sex and the African American gay experience. This is what I bought the book for as it sounds incredibly interesting. However, after reading it and being completely underwhelmed I joked with friends that I have written better one-handed poetry and my sexual adventures are a lot more cringy than his!!

The more we joked about it the more I thought why not? People are self-publishing their one-handed romances, their one-handed erotica, and their one-handed poetry all the time now. Why not me?

I know it's bad. I know it's angsty as only a 20-year old's poetry about love and sex can be angsty.

And if you leave a one-star rating. I completely understand.

Explicit Scenes from Gay Pulps and MM Romances:
Including biased opinions from Gene Rusco, pseudo-intellectual

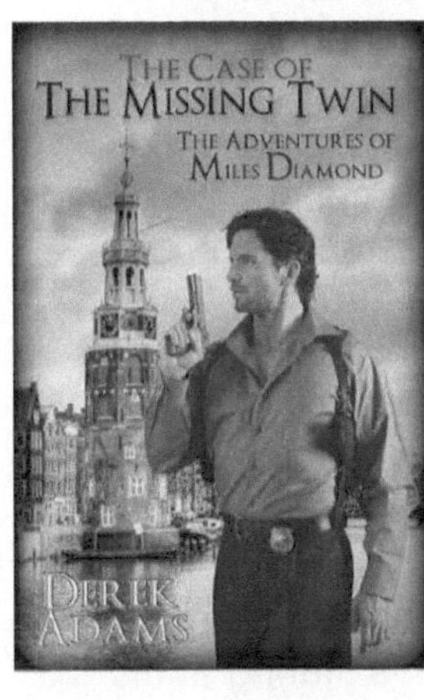

The Case of the Missing Twin by Derek Adams published by Extasy Books, a republished edition in 2013 and originally published by the pulp publisher Badboy in 1993.

Blurb: "The erotic adventures of intrepid detective Miles Diamond kick off with *The Case of the Missing Twin*. Miles is a genius in the bedroom, although he is often at a loss when it comes to solving crimes. Unwilling to let his limitations stand in his way, Miles constantly finds himself in a variety of compromising positions with a cast of randy studs—each of whom harbors a secret of two of his own. Miles diligently sets about uncovering everything within reach as he tracks down the elusive and delectable Daniel Travis."

Excerpt: "He shucked off his coat and pulled his shirt up over his succulent pecs. On the left side, just above a big pinkish brown nipple, was a strawberry birthmark, shaped vaguely like a heart, no other distinguishing scars set his body apart from any other of the examples of physical perfection I'd ogled over the years, but the view was a pleasant one. My eyes wandered down over his flat belly–I could think of several moves that would tense it up like a washboard.

He turned around slowly and pushed his pants down to his knees. A tiny pink handprint, no bigger than a quarter stared up at me from his right cheek, quivering slightly when he shifted his weight. Without even thinking, I reached out and caressed his sleek ass. He looked over his shoulder and winked at me, at the same time thrusting his butt back in what seemed an open invitation. I petted him again and he practically purred. It was all the encouragement I needed. I dropped to my knees to have another look at the telltale mark.

My aim must not have been good as I thought, because, next thing I knew, I was staring at his quivering rosebud of an asshole. Fine golden hairs ringed it, lying flat and damp against his cheeks. I flicked my tongue along his crack, pausing to tease the tight pucker on my way down to his big fuzzy balls. He pushed back against my face with a smack and I gave in to the impulse to play hide and seek with my tongue. He bent over, spread his cheeks, and opened wide... I jammed my tongue in right up to the root, reaching between his legs, grabbed his hard prick and used it to hold his butt against my face. With my free hand, I fumbled with my belt and zipper and released my cock from the confines of my pants. It popped up like a flagpole, already starting to drool.

I rimmed his tight butt voraciously, nipping gently at his sweet little ass lips from time to time. Judging by the way that he was writhing around after a few minutes of this treatment I figured he was ready for a change of pace. I gave him a couple of farewell licks, stood up, grabbed his golden mane, bent him over at the waist and pointed my cock at paradise.

I watched in amazement as he rammed himself back to my short-and-curlies in one brusque move. No need for warm-ups here. I grabbed him by the waist and went at it top speed–pulling out til his ass ring was just grabbing me by the crown, then slamming back til my balls bounced against his. David braced his arms on the back of the couch, legs spread wide. I was pounding him so hard that his head bounced against the wall every time I drove home, but he was still begging for more. Finally, my balls snapped up in a knot and I squirted cum up into him til he drolled out around the base of my prick and splattered on the bare floor of my office.

Ever the gentleman, I reached between his legs to help him out as soon as I caught my breath. His dick flexed against my palm, filling my hand with hot juice before I'd done a dozen strokes. When he came his ass ring clamped down on me like a vise– if it'd had teeth, I would've been in trouble.

He pulled off me, sprawled back on the couch and grabbed his ankles, lifting his legs and spreading them wide. "This time around, I want to watch you fuck me. I want to see your big prick slipping in and out of me."

He leered at me, sweat beading on his upper lip. I leered right back, dropped to my knees and took aim once again." pgs 15-17.

B.O. I truly do not understand the point of modern pulp novels. If I want porn, I can watch porn. I do not read novels with my dick out jerking off as I read. Readers are heard saying they enjoy graphic sex scenes as long as it is important to the story. Knowing they had sex is usually all we need to know. How and how hard they fucked does not add to a story. Nor do I need to know how big one's cock is.

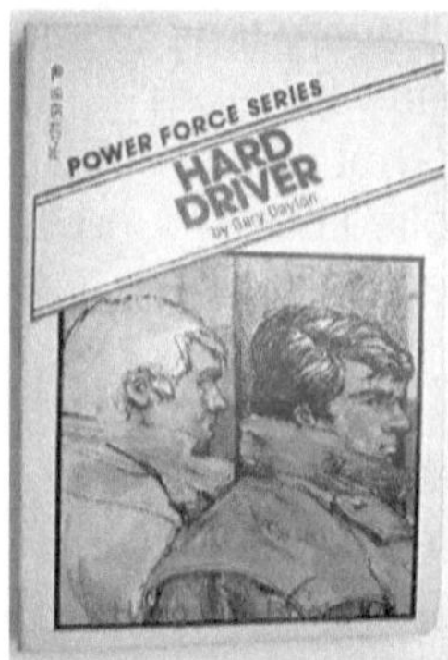

Hard Driver by Gary Dayton published by Arena Publications in 1987, originally published in 1984. This is a reprint and the name Gary Dayton is a company name shared by many different authors.

Excerpt:: "He felt the sudden heat from the old man's palm, and the urgent pressure.

"You're a beautiful young man, Bernie."

"Please, Doctor. Let's not do something you'll be sorry for later."

The professor laughed lightly, "sorry, Bernie. I'm never sorry to share a little youth. It keeps me vigorous."

The doctor had gripped Bernie's cock, and he was slowly masterbating the hardening length. "D-doctor…I'm not… I'm not really interested."

"That's my job, isn't it? To make you interested."

"Doctor, no."

But the skin of his cock was being jerked rapidly now, and he knew he was giving in to it. His prick gorged itself with sudden blood and rose within the firm palm, thickening and throbbing. The rosy head oozed from the taut folds of fingers and protruded upward, the glans swelling and distending with each downward thrust of Floyd's hand.

"You could make a fortune," the older gushed. "A fortune, Bernie. There are hundreds and hundreds of lonely old men like me who'd pay dearly to do this, to touch your exciting body…and to do *this*, Bernie."

He went slowly down to his knees, and Bernie saw the long old cock that had been so straight and flaccid begin to rise and arc outward from the soft gray folds of belly flesh and salt and pepper public hair. Floyd had life in him yet. A great deal of vigor, as he called it. Bernie could feel his breath on his cock, lips close to the urethra and begging for entry, tongue flicking out in short, quick seizures of desire to kiss the eye of the wand. Bernie tried to push him away gently.

"Don't do this, Doctor Cartwright. Don't lower yourself this way."

"I'm not lowering myself, Bernie. I'm elevating my emotions. Do you really think this is the first time? I feel *young*, Bernie, by savoring the young."

"But…but you could lose your job."

He felt the pursing of the lips around his cockhead and the slow glide of the moist mouth over it and off again. "Really Bernie, enjoy it."
"I can't. I can't let you do this. It isn't right…a man like you."

Gently Floyd Cartwright pumped life continually into Bernie's rapidly inflating cock. And with his free hand he cupped the hairy balls against his face and rolled them gently against his chin and against the cockstem that touched his lips. He could smell the musky odor he desired so deeply. "A man like me," he murmured."A lonely old man like me. I live for a moment such as this. How I envy old Oscar Wilde, who could wander down onto the docks of London or into the back reaches of the city and take muscular cocks of the sun, great huge men with timbers before them, and steal their sweet juice that otherwise would have gone down the sweaty sewer of some tuppence doxy."

He kissed Bernie's cock, and dragged his lips the length of it, feeling sudden throbbings that shook the length to the root and contracted the balls in his hands; felt the sperm alive and anxious for his throat. He gulped.

"And Auden," he said, "who could walk a street and spot some incredibly well-hung gutter stud and take him home to tea and write a poem to him while he blew him, even as the delicious cum poured from the spout and down his throat. A beautiful, gracious poem full of as much music as he found in the hard body of that noble stallion. He could have blown a horse, Bernie, as he wrote *A Day for a Lay*, Bernie. Give me your pipe and let me smoke it. Let me inhale the sweet tars, the white tars of your soul. Give me joy, Bernie, like you're built to bestow as surely as knighthood on a serf."

His words were almost hypnotic to Bernie as his long cock undulated to the ravaging tongue and lips and words.

"Someone will find out," Bernie said weakly…

"I know the look, Bernie. I read it in your face. This isn't the virginal march for you. I know you've had men. I only ask my turn in line."

He could feel Floyd's tongue lapping at the stiff hairs, and then around his balls and over the tender reaches of perineal flesh, then down the quivering thighs. Bernie didn't fight any longer. He put his fingers in the old professor's hair and kneaded his scalp, closed his eyes.

"Come into me know," the professor gasped, tonguing the undercarriage from the base to the tip, licking the deep ethereal eye.

"Eat me," Bernie gasped, and he felt the lips part around him, and the gradually increasing pressure and heat as his hard cock slipped into the tight throat, the cradle of all his momentary adventures. His cock explored, dug deeply.

"*Swallow* it," Bernie moaned, beginning to move his hips, thrusting cautiously against the old man's face. He felt he warm hands come around and massage his ass, felt the fingers easing between his buttocks and finding the hole, felt a thick forefinger as urgent as a cock stretching his asshole, invading him, fucking him, and it was delicious. He began a quick and sudden fucking motion, thrusting deeply into Floyd's throat, imprisoning himself, gorging the old man's gullet with a bombardment that rocked Floyd's ass back and forth. Bernie could feel the gripping of his ass for support, and, as if he wanted to prove something to this old man he seized Floyd's ears, painfully he knew, though Floyd didn't groan. Je whimpered with pleasure as the hard elasticity of the swollen cock gored him again and again, rapidly like the swift drift of a well-oiled piston, a dynamo, rhythmic, buttocks tensing and dimpling as Bernie's musculature strained to the fuck. Again and again the air gushed from the professor's mouth and around the cock, *umph, umph, umph, umph.* Tears were trickling from the old man's eye, his head back to give the prick the proper angle of thrust. He took it deeply into his throat, swallowing and gulping the head as it swept past the opening to his throat and down and down. And he gulped and sucked and slurped on the outward stroke. *Umphf, unh, umphf.* He needed air, and he let the throbbing hose slip from his lips and flop around his cheeks, while he gulped the precious oxygen, then fiercely he was on the root again, groveling downward greedily, huskily, until his nose was buried in Bernie's hair the big balls were smacking against his chin. Not once did Bernie cease his

thumping heaves upward into the hot mouth. He
was groaning, growling with passion as he thumped
inch after inch into the old man. He felt his knees
growing weak as the orgasm approached. Floyd's
hands left his buttocks, sensing the dying gasp of
the young man's body, and thrust upward over his
back and down his sides, clawing gently at the
excited flesh. He could feel Bernie's weight coming
forward over him, and he let his body go with the
weight until he was lying flat on the tiled floor, his
face covered fully by the rippling muscles of the
young lover's bounding body. The pubic hair
swirled over his eyes, and the balls spilled around
his throat, battering him as Bernie's body bucked
and thrust, bucked and thrust into him. *Umphf,
umphf, umphf.* The bathroom rang with the sound
of sucking…and gasps…sighs and grains and
growls of sex that approached rage. Bernie mewled
the words and spoke them strongly to the mirror.
He could see his face struck with emotion, and he
closed his eyes suddenly as the first grab of the
tunnel hit him, and his sperm rocketed from the
balls and into the old man's throat. He heard the
shock, the gulp, the swallowing as spurt after spurt
of his hot cum struck the mouth's hot walls. He
pushed deeper, deeper, ground into the old man's
throat until Floyd's excitement overwhelmed him
and he almost gagged, spewing some of the cum
from his lips and down his chin.

End excerpt. The young man then rides the
professor's cock until he too cums. "Never had
Bernie felt so full."

B. O. I have no idea how many people were in the
room. Is the doctor, the professor, and Floyd the

same person? And I seriously can't read Bernie without thinking of Bernie Sanders which really makes this scene even more disturbing.

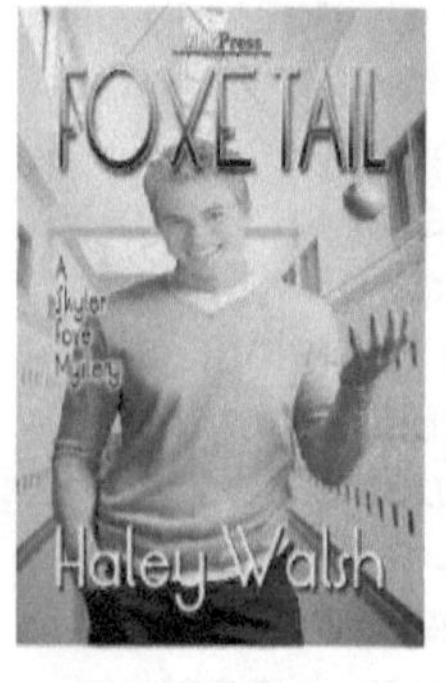

Foxe Tail by Haley Walsh published by MLR Press in 2010. This was the first mm romance novels I read. I did not know that there was a genre called mm romance at the time. I read it. The mystery was decent but the sex scenes were so unrealistic that it had me laughing at times. Fortunately as the series progressed the sex scenes declined… That or I started skipping them altogether.

After Walsh published the last book in the series she announced that it would be the last book in the series because apparently people do not like to read long series… Ummm… Sue Grafton wrote 25 books in the Alphabet series, James Patterson has a lot of long series lasting into the 20s, 30s, and even 40s, and JD Robb has a series into the 40s. Don't blame readers if your books stop selling.

Blurb: "Skyler Foxe is a brand new English teacher in his hometown of Redlands, CA. He loves literature, loves his students, loves his friends, especially his best friend Detective Sidney Feldman. But he doesn't love keeping his orientation a secret, afraid of the backlash in this conservative county. But will murder thrust him into unwanted limelight? Who killed his principal's son outside a gay dance club? And what's the connection to James Polk High? Is the macho football coach or his mysterious and gorgeous new assistant coach involved? Can Skyler trust anyone at the high school when there seems to be conspiracies around every corner?

Excerpt: "Skyler smiled at him. The Viking smiled back, a wide, friendly and quite frankly *sexy* smile. *Oh Skyler, you are about to get sooo lucky.* Skyler danced toward him and the Viking moved in Skyler's direction. Suddenly they were dancing in front of each other. The Viking put his arms over Skyler's shoulders and moved in, grating his hips. "Aren't you just adorable," he said, voice deep and smooth.

Skyler melted. "Thanks. And *you* are hot."

The man smiled again, white teeth against tan skin and blond curls around his face. His mouth was plump and sensuous. There had to be a law. The Viking leaned forward and gace Skyler a soft kiss on his lips. *And he kisses too,* thought Skyler, vibrating with pleasure.

He looked Skyler up and down. "Do you live nearby?"

"Yeah. Only a few blocks. Wanna go?"

…

Skyler unlocked his door and flipped on the bedroom light and took off his shirt. He toed off his shoes just as the doorbell rang. He hopped through the living room, getting rid of his socks one at a time, and punched in some music. Barry White crooned "Never Gonna Give You Up." He reached the door breathless as the music played softly behind him. The Viking leaned in the doorway. Delicious.

"Come on in," said Skyler.

The man looked around in a cursory fashion, not really interested in the room. He scooped up Skyler in his brawny arms and pressed his open mouth to Skyler's, snaking in his tongue. They kissed, lips clasping tightly, until the man drew back. "What's your name, pretty boy?"

…

They both soon divested themselves of trousers and slipped off their briefs. But when Skyler looked down at Jim's erection he stopped dead. *Holy Shit!*

The Viking was pierced. And not just a little. He had a silver Prince Albert through his glans, and running down the underside of his prick was a Frenum Ladder of four posts.

...

"Haven't you ever been fucked by a guy with piercings?"

"Not on their—in your—Holy shit. How do you—you know. How do you get a condom on?"
"It's not a problem." Jim leaned forward, eyes half-closed. "I've been told it's very invigorating."

"I'll bet."

"But we'll get to that in a minute. I'm not in any rush." Jim slip down to his knees, cupped his hands over Skyler's ass, and wrapped hi warm lips around his dick.

Wet heat. That was the feeling of lips and tongue flicking and slithering over his cock. He ran his hands through Jim's long hair and bucked, but strong fingers digging his ass cheeks kept him in check. The Viking drew back and licked up the length of his cock, teasing he ridge with the tip of his tongue before swirling it over the slit and slurping up the pre-cum. He smiled and engulfed him again, humming in pleasure as he suckled. With one hand firmly on Skyler's ass cheeks, he reached back with the other and gently fondled Skyler's scrotum, giving it just the slightest squeeze.

Skyler had been on edge and hadn't realized how much he needed this, especially as his balls drew up with aching need. Up on his toes, he tugged on Jim's hair to give him warning and Jim smiled around his dick before sucking deeply. That was all it took and Skyler unloaded with a gasp.

Jim held him for a moment, licking gently at his sensitive balls before Skyler's wobbly knees gave out. He leaned forward and kissed Jim's soft mouth before urging him over to the bed and pushing him down to a sitting position. Skyler sank to his knees and swallowed the thick, red dick whole, feeling the cold strangeness of the various steel studs on his tongue. Skyler always appreciated a well-hung man, and Jim was certainly a champion. Skyler stroked with his tongue and drew his lips up and down Jim's meat, sucking hard on the up side. The man's orgasm was sudden and worth it. He growled and pumped his hips and released a truly spectacular load. Skyler almost choked but managed to slurp it down. There was nothing like an energetic lover.

Jim grabbed Skyler, dragged him up to the bed, and curled him under his brawny arms, kissing him deeply. They napped for a while before round two. This time Skyler helped him sheath his studded dick with a condom and maneuvered on top, sliding down carefully and feeling each stud as it passed his rim.

"Holy shit," he murmured and Jim hummed some more as he muzzled Skyler's neck. He held Skyler's butt in place and gently raised and lowered him. Skyler held onto Jim's arms but soon slid his fingers to his beefy neck and started riding hard. The studs did the trick on his prostate and his fingers around his own cock did the rest."

End excerpt. Pages 111-114.

B. O. I skipped past boring sections where Skyler gave Jim instructions to his house, where they introduced themselves, and where Skyler said "Holy Shit," a bunch of times about the studs.

Lay Your Sleeping Head by Michael Nava.

This one kills me having to include it. I love Michael Nava's works. His Henry Rios series was amazing but in 2016 he decided he wanted to rewrite *The Little Death* for a wider audience and so included graphic sex scenes to appeal to the readers of MM romance and renamed it *Lay Your Sleeping Head*.

The original book had few sex scenes and definitely no on page sex. Having read the rewritten work it makes me wonder if Michael Nava is indeed gay. The sex is awkwardly written and feels unnatural and forced.

Blurb: Thirty years ago, *The Little Death* introduced Henry Rios, a gay, Latino criminal defense lawyer who became the central figure in a celebrated seven novel series. In a brilliant reimagination of *The Little Death*, *Lay Your Sleeping Head* retains all the complexity and elegance of the plot of the original novel but deepens the themes of personal alienation and erotic obsession that both honored the traditions of the American crime novel and turned them on their head. Henry Rios, a gifted and humane lawyer driven to drink by professional failure and personal demons, meets a charming junky struggling to stay clean. He tells Rios an improbable tale of long-ago murders in his wealthy family. Rios is skeptical, but the erotic spark between them ignites an obsessive affair that ends only when the man's body is discovered with a

needle in his arm on the campus of a great
California university. Rios refuses to believe his
lover's death was an accidental overdose. His hunt
for the killer takes him down San Francisco's mean
streets and into Nob Hill mansions where he
uncovers the secrets behind a legendary California

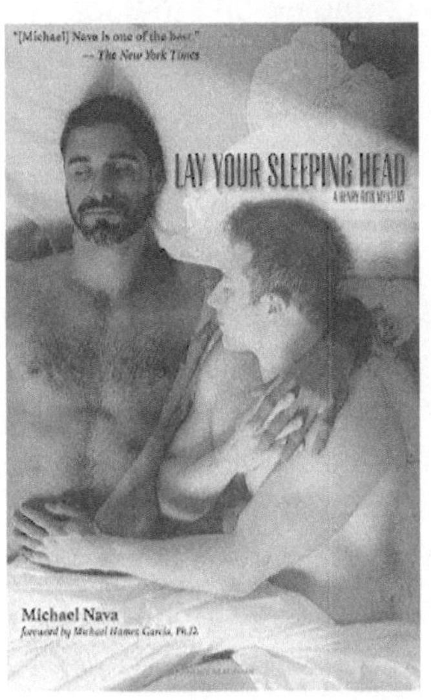

fortune and the reason
the man he loved had to
die.

Before I type the excerpt,
I want to touch on the
cover. Being somewhat in
the publishing industry I
know that authors don't
always get what they
want when it comes to
their covers. Sometimes
they lament that fact and
sometimes it is for their
own good.

Michael Nava really liked this cover. And it's fine
but Henry Rios always surprises his lovers when he
takes his shirt off for the first time as his chest and
stomach are completely hairless. Yet, here is a
model representing Henry Rios who has a very
hairy chest.

But I digress.

Excerpt:

I woke up alone and watched the shadow of the tree outside sway across the wall. The only noises were the clock ticking and the wind. The sheets and blankets were kicked back and over the foot of the bed. A wadded up towel lay crumpled on the floor among Hugh's scattered clothes.

I could still taste him in my mouth, ripe, meaty, musky. Armpits, anus, cock. My stomach was glazed with his semen, the sheets were stained with mine. Like everything else about him, sex was compelling and off-kilter. What started as the standard one-night-stand groping and negotiations quickly became something more serious.

"Use me," he told me, when I had tumbled him to his back and parted his legs. "That's how I like it."

There was always that moment when I was grappling naked with another man that our bodies veered toward violence; it was part of the excitement of the encounter that these tough, male bodies capable of inflicting injury on each other would, instead, become instruments of pleasure. The line could be very fine…. [they fall asleep]

He rolled off of me, opened the drawer and removed the tube of KY Jelly. He straddled my thighs, squeezed a gob on his finger and his hand disappeared behind his body. He smirked as he coated his hole with the lube. I reached up and traced the ridged muscles of his belly with my fingertips.

"You are so beautiful."

"You are, Henry."

He squeezed another thick drop of lube on his fingers and slowly spread it up and down my shaft. I squirmed beneath the cold jelly and his fingers.

"I'm going to ride you," he said. "That okay?"

I managed a weak, "uh huh."

He lifted his thighs, scooted up my body, positioned my cock against his hole and then, mouth slightly ajar, his eyes locked on mine, slowly lowered himself. The tight muscle gave way, stretching to take me in.

"Oh fuck," I whispered, as the cock penetrated the sticky heat of his anus. Arush of blood prickled my chest and belly; my groin pulsed sweetness.

Hugh's mouth was an O, his eyes clouded with pleasure. For a moment, he remained motionless, his butt on my thighs, his hands on my chest. Then, he began to move up and down on my cock, slowly fucking himself on me. I thrust upward in response.

"No, he said. "Let me take care of you."

I nodded and lay back. Expertly, he impaled himself on me, varying the speed and depth of the strokes, tightening and relaxing his hold around my cock as he did. He watched me, smiling when I moaned, shaking his head when I couldn't help thrusting. Translucent threads of precum spilled from his cock to my belly. I reached for it, massaged the head with the stickiness. Gently, he moved my hand away. "This is all about you," he said. I surrendered and lay back, closed my eyes and slipped into the swamp of sensations, smells and sounds of sex; his butt rising and falling on my sweaty thighs, the bursts of breath and involuntary moans, the fire in my engorged cock responding to the heat and friction as he pounded himself on me. When I stuttered, "I'm coming," he slowed the pace, squeezing my cock with his hole, and when I came, it wasn't in a hot gush, but a slow flood that curled my toes.

When the last pulse of my semen emptied into his gut, he grabbed his cock. A few rapid strokes brought an arc of cum that splattered my chest and chin.

End excerpt. Pages 26-21.

B. O. Other than the awkward phrasing I mostly want to comment on the last paragraph. As Henry emptied his semen into Hugh's gut. Ummm, does

Michael Nava not understand anatomy? Cumming into one's ass does not lead semen to the stomach. Trust me as a mostly bottom that after being cummed into, one needs to be close to a bathroom within a couple hours after sex to make sure it doesn't just drain out at an unfortunate moment.

I want to discuss cover images again. Jay B Laws wrote the books *Steam* and *The Unfinished*. He disliked the cover of *Steam* and recommended another picture instead. The cartoonish cover (in a really gaudy pink) was the cover Alyson Press went with whereas Laws really wanted the cover to be him in a shower with lots of steam. I honestly think the image of him in the shower would have sold more copies for sure!

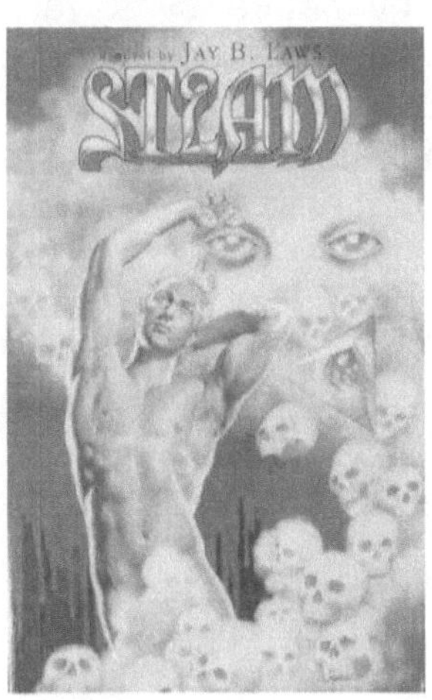

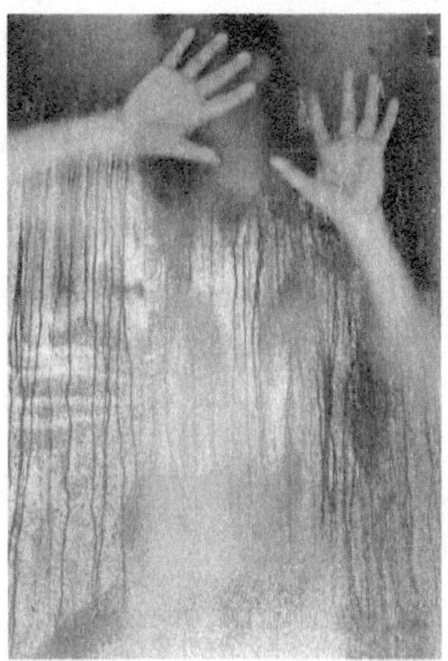

RECOLLECTIONS OF A MARY-ANN[1]

—:o:—

INTRODUCTION

The writer of these notes was walking through Leicester Square one sunny afternoon last November, when his attention was particularly taken by an effeminate, but very good-looking young fellow, who was walking in front of him, looking in shop-windows from time to time, and now and then looking round as if to attract my attention.

Dressed in tight-fitting clothes, which set off his Adonis-like figure to the best advantage, especially about what snobs call the fork of his trousers, where evidently he was favoured by nature by a very extraordinary development of the male appendages; he had small and elegant feet, set off by pretty patent leather boots, a fresh looking beardless face, with almost feminine features, auburn hair, and sparkling blue eyes, which spoke as plainly as possible to my senses, and told me that the handsome youth must indeed be one of the "Mary-Ann's" of London, who I had heard were often to be seen sauntering in the neighbourhood of Regent Street, or the Haymarket, on fine afternoons or evenings.

Presently the object of my curiosity almost halted and stood facing the writer as he took off his hat, and

---

[1] A Mary Ann was a male prostitute during the Victorian Age.

wiped his face with a beautiful white silk handkerchief.

That lump in his trousers had quite a fascinating effect upon me. Was it natural or made up by some artificial means? If real, what a size when excited; how I should like to handle such a manly jewel, etc. All this ran through my mind, and determined me to make his acquaintance, in order to unravel the real and naked truth; also, if possible, to glean what I could of his antecedents and mode of life, which I felt sure must be extraordinarily interesting.

When he moved on again I noticed that he turned down a little side street, and was looking in a picture shop. I followed him, and first making some observations about the scanty drapery on some of the actresses and other beauties whose photographs were exposed for sale, I asked him if he would take a glass of wine.

He appeared to comprehend that there was business in my proposal, but seemed very diffident about drinking in any public place.

"Well," I said, "would you mind if we take a cab to my chambers—I live in the Cornwall Mansions, close to Baker Street Station—have a cigar and a chat with me, as I see you are evidently a fast young chap, and can put me up to a thing or two?"

"All right. Put your thing up, I suppose you mean. Why do you seem so afraid to say what you want?" he replied with a most meaning look.

"I'm not at all delicate; but wish to keep myself out of trouble. Who can tell who hears you out in the streets?" I said, hailing a cab. "I don't like to be seen speaking to a young fellow in the street. We shall be all right in my own rooms."

It was just about my dinner hour when we reached my place, so I rang the bell, and ordered my old housekeeper to lay the table for two, and both of us did ample justice to a good rumpsteak and oyster sauce, topped up with a couple of bottles of champagne of an extra sec brand.

As soon as the cloth was removed, we settled ourselves comfortably over the fire with brandy and cigars, for it was a sharp, frosty day out.

"My boy, I hope you enjoyed your dinner?" I said, mixing a couple of good warm glasses of brandy hot, "but you have not favoured me with your name. Mine you could have seen by the little plate on my door, is Mr. Cambon."

"Saul, Jack Saul, sir, of Lisle Street, Leicester Square, and ready for a lark with a free gentleman at any time. What was it made you take a fancy to me? Did you observe any particularly interesting points about your humble servant?" as he slyly looked down towards the prominent part I have previously mentioned.

"You seem a fine figure, and so evidently well hung that I had quite a fancy to satisfy my curiosity about it. Is it real or made up for show?" I asked.

"As real as my face, sir, and a great deal prettier. Did you ever see a finer tosser in your life?" he replied, opening his trousers and exposing a tremendous prick, which was already in a half-standing state. "It's my only fortune, sir; but it really provides for all I want, and often introduces me to the best of society, ladies as well as gentlemen. There isn't a girl about Leicester Square but what would like to have me for her man, but I find it more to my interest not to waste my strength on women; the pederastic game pays so well, and is quite as enjoyable. I wouldn't have a woman unless well paid for it."

He was gently frigging himself as he spoke, and had a glorious stand by the time he had finished, so throwing the end of my cigar into the fire, I knelt down by his side to examine that fine plaything of his.

Opening his trousers more, I brought everything into full view—a priapus nearly ten inches long, very thick, and underhung by a most glorious pair of balls, which were surrounded and set off by quite a profusion of light auburn curls.

How I handled those appendages, the sack of which was drawn up so deliciously tight, which is a sure sign of strength, and that they have not been enervated by too excessive fucking or frigging. I hate to see balls hang loosely down, or even a fine prick with very small or scarcely any stones to it— these half-and-half tools are an abomination.

Gently frigging him, I tongued the ruby head for a minute or two, till he called out, "Hold, hold, sir, or you will get it in your mouth!"

This was not my game; I wanted to see him spend, so removing my lips, I pointed that splendid tool outwards over the hearthrug and frigged him quickly. Almost in a moment it came; first a single thick clot was ejected, like a stone from a volcano, then quite a jet of sperm went almost a yard high, and right into the fire, where it fizzled on the red-hot coals.

"By Jove, what a spend!" I exclaimed, "we will strip now, and have some better fun, Jack. I want to see you completely naked, my boy, as there is nothing so delightful as to see a fine young fellow when well formed and furnished in every respect. Will you suck me? That is what I like first; frigging you has only given me half a cockstand at present."

"You must be generous if I do, or you will not get me to come and see you here again," he answered with a smile, which had almost a girlish sweetness of expression.

We were soon stripped to the buff, and having locked the door, I sat down with my beautiful youth on my knee, we kissed each other, and he thrust his tongue most wantonly into my mouth, as my hands fairly travelled all over his body; but that glorious prick of his claimed most attention, and I soon had it again in a fine state of erection.

"Now kneel down and gamahuche me," I said, "whilst I can frig your lovely prick with my foot."

Seemingly to enter thoroughly into the spirit of the thing, he was on his knees in a moment, between my legs, and began to fondle my still rather limp pego most deliciously, taking the head fully into his voluptuously warm mouth, and rolling his tongue round the prepuce in the most lascivious manner it is possible to imagine.

I stiffened up at once under such exciting tittillations, which seemed to have a like effect upon his prick, which I could feel with my toes to be as hard as a rolling-pin, as my foot gently frigged and rolled it on his bended thigh, and he soon spent over my sole as it gently continued the exciting friction.

I now gave myself more and more to his gamahuching, now and then seizing his head with both hands, and raising his face to mine, we indulged in luscious love kisses, which prolonged my pleasure almost indefinitely. At last I allowed him to bring me to a crisis, and he swallowed every drop of my spendings with evident relish.

After resting awhile, and taking a little more stimulant, I asked him how he had come to acquire such a decided taste for gamahuching, to do it so deliciously as he did.

"That would be too long a tale to go into now," he replied. "Some other day, if you like to make it worth my while, I will give you the whole history."

"Could you write it out, or give me an outline so that I might put it into the shape of a tale?"

"Certainly; but it would take me so much time that you would have to make me a present of at least twenty pounds. It would take during three or four weeks several hours a day."

"I don't mind a fiver a week if you give me a fair lot, say thirty or forty pages of note-paper a week, tolerably well written," I replied.

And the arrangement was made for him to compile me "The Recollections of a Mary-Ann," which I suggested ought to be the title, although he seemed not at all to like the name as applied to himself, saying that that was what the low girls of his neighbourhood called him if they wished to insult him, however, he said at last, "the four fivers will make up for that."

"Now," he added, "I suppose you would like me to put it up for you, or rather into myself. But can you lend me such a thing as a birch? You are not so young as I am, and want something to stimulate you; besides, I want you to do it well, as I fancy that moderate sized cock of yours immensely. Do you know that I am sure I like a nice man to fuck me as much as ever a woman could?"

The birch was produced, and he insisted upon tying me down over the easy chair, so that I could not flinch or get away from the application of the rod.

He began very steadily, and with light stinging cuts which soon made me aware that I had a rather accomplished young schoolmaster to deal with my posteriors, which began to tingle most pleasantly after a few strokes. The sting of each cut was sharp, but the warm, burning rush of blood to the parts had such an exciting effect that, although I fairly writhed and wriggled under each stroke, I was rapidly getting into a most delicious state of excitement.

The light tips of the birch seemed to search out each tender spot, twining round my buttocks and thighs, touching up both shaft and balls, as well as wealing my ham, till I was most rampantly erect, and cried out for him to let me have him at once.

"Not yet; not yet, you bugger. You want to get into my arse, do you? I'll teach you to fuck arseholes, my boy!" he exclaimed, chuckling over my mingled pain and excitement.

"How do you like that—and that—and that—and that?" The last stroke was so painful that it almost took my breath away, and I knew he had fairly drawn blood.

I was furious, my prick felt red-hot, almost ready to burst, when he unloosed my hands and ancles.

I seized him in a perfect fury of lust. His prick was also standing like a bar of iron; he had got so excited by my flagellation. He was turned round, and made to kneel upon the chair at once, presenting his bottom to my attack. No one to look at it would have thought the pinky and wrinkled little hole had ever been much used, except for the necessary offices of nature. The sight was perfectly maddening; it looked so delicious.

As I stopped for a moment to lubricate the head of my prick with saliva, he put his fingers in his mouth, and then wetted the little hole himself, to make it as easy as possible for me.

Coming to the charge, I found him delightfully tight, but I got in slowly as he helped me as much as possible by directing the head of my cock with his hand, whilst I had him round the waist and handled that beautiful tool of his, which added immensely to my pleasure. At last I felt fairly in, but did not want to spend too soon, so only moved very slowly, enjoying the sense of possession and the delicious pressures which he evidently so well knew how to apply.

My frigging soon brought him to a spend, and catching it all in my hands, I rubbed the creamy essence of life up and down his prick and over his balls, and even on my own cock as it drew in and out of his bottom.

My delight was perfectly indescribable. I drew it out so long, always stopping for a little when the spending crisis seemed imminent, but at last his writhings and pressures had such an irresistible effect that I could no longer restrain the flood of sperm I had tried so long to keep back, and feeling it shoot from me in a red-hot stream, the agonizing delight made both of us give vent to perfect howls of extasy.

We both nearly fainted, but my instrument was so hard and inflamed that it was a long time before it in the least began to abate its stiffness.

It was still in his bottom, revelling in the well-lubricated hole, and he would fain have worked me up to the very crisis again, but I was afraid of exhausting myself too much at one time, so gradually allowed Mr. Pego to assume his normal size, and slip out of that delicious orifice which had given me such pleasure.

A week after this first introduction Jack came again, and brought the first instalment of his rough notes, from which this MS. is compiled.

Of course at each visit we had a delicious turn at bottom-fucking, but as the recital of the same kind of thing over and over again is likely to pall upon my readers, I shall omit a repetition of our numerous orgies of lust, all very similar to the foregoing, and content myself by a simple recital of his adventures.

JACK SAUL'S RECOLLECTIONS

EARLY DEVELOPMENT OF THE

PEDERASTIC IDEAS IN HIS

YOUTHFUL MIND

DEAR SIR,—

I need scarcely tell you that little cocks, and everything relating to them, had a peculiar interest to me from the very earliest time it is possible for my memory to carry me back to.

I have a brother much older than myself, and have heard him say that almost as soon as I could walk I would toddle up to anybody and ask them if they had a dilly; that lifting girls' clothes, or putting my hands on boys or even grown-up people was a regular thing with me.

My parents were well-to-do people of the farmer class, in Suffolk, and I have been told of a laughable incident when I was only about six years old.

There was a family party, and at teatime my cousin Jenny, a fine girl of about seventeen, who was slightly disfigured by a very hirsute appearance about her upper lip, was seated opposite to me, and particularly attracted my attention, it being the first time I had ever seen her. I was so absorbed in contemplating her moustache that I could not take my eyes off her, so that she quite blushed.

At last I broke out. "What have you got girl's clothes on for? I don't believe you are a girl at all. My brother Dick has got a moustache just like yours."

"Hush, for shame, Johnny; be quiet, do," said my mother, giving me quite a severe pat, whilst the object of my remarks flushed crimson, as tears of shame started to her eyes.

"I won't. I know she's a boy. See if I don't find out whether she's cracked like a girl, or got a spout like a tea-kettle on her!" I cried out, but was not allowed to say more, as I was cuffed and driven in disgrace from the room, whilst poor Jenny also rose from the table to retire and have a good cry over her humiliation.

About twelve years afterwards, when Jenny was a married woman, happening to be left alone with her for a short time one day, I recalled the incident to her memory, in fact I believe she never forgot it, as she used always to regard me with a most peculiar kind of look.

How she blushed at first; but putting my arms round her waist, I asked her to kiss and forgive me, if it was such a long time ago.

"You know, Jack, I will. You were such a tit then," she replied, as she permitted me to take the kiss.

"But, Jenny, I love you so, and am as curious as ever. Can you forgive that?"

Her eyes looked anywhere but in my face, as she blushed and seemed deeply moved, so I redoubled my osculatory attentions till I had raised quite a storm of desire in both our heaving bosoms.

She was married to a rather old and ugly fellow, whose money had caught the silly butterfly, who thought that wealth alone could secure happiness.

You may guess the result. A friendly sofa was at hand. We sank down upon it, and, in spite of her pretended resistance, I not only investigated the crack of love but got into it. She was one of those hairy, lustful women one occasionally meets with, and when she had once tasted the fine root I introduced into her cunt (which was already swimming in spendings before Mr. Pego could present his head), she could scarcely ever be satisfied; in fact, we ran awful risks. When I was stopping in the house she would leave her husband asleep and come to my room, and when she had fairly fucked me to a standstill, would suck my prick, slap my arse, bugger me with her finger, and do everything she could think of to get even a tenth or eleventh go out of me.

I was sent to a boarding-school at Colchester when about ten years of age. Here the boys all slept by twos in a bed.

Well do I remember the first night. My bedfellow, a big boy of about fifteen, his name was Freeman, at once began to handle me all over as soon as the lights were out. His hands soon found my cock, which young as I then was, was a fine one for my age—somehow it was already stiff.

"My eyes," he whispered, "you've got a good 'un. Feel mine; it is hardly bigger than yours," as he directed my young hands to another equally stiff prick.

"Rub it up and down," he whispered again; "that is what we all do. Do you like it?"

My body was in a tremble all over, and presently, as I continued the up and down motion of my hand on his cock, it was wetted all over with a warm, slimy kind of stuff which he shot into my hand.

"Don't you know what that is, Jack? Perhaps you're not old enough to come like that; we call it spendings," he whispered. "It's so nice. We often put our cocks in each other's bottoms, and spend there. Would you like to try that on me?"

At first I would not, but he at length got me to promise and try, as I should be sure to find it so nice.

He turned his bum to me, and wetting both his hole and the tip of my affair with spittle, he himself directed my cock to the place, and pushed out his arse towards me.

I did my best by shoving, and somehow it seemed to come quite natural, for I soon got in, and found my prick for the first time in a deliciously moist, warm, and tight sheath.

"Push in and out, in and out," he whispered, suiting the action of his rump to his instructions.

I liked it immensely, and clung with my arms round his buttocks, working with all my will, till at last a sudden thrill seemed to come upon me with a kind of shooting sensation in my cock. We both stopped out of breath, as if something had happened, and I suppose that was my first spend.

The other boys seemed all very quiet that first night, but the next evening, as soon as we had retired to our room, Freeman at once introduced little Jack to the other half-dozen occupants of our room (there were four beds) as a highly fit and proper chum.

"See, boys, what a fine prick the little fellow has got. He fucked my arse all night last night, and had his first spend," he said, lifting my shirt and exposing my affair, which was already as stiff as a poker at the idea of another go like the previous night.

They all crowded round to handle and admire what they called a wonder for such a little 'un.

Presently all were quite naked, each prick was stiff, and we compared one with another. The next thing was to draw lots who should have my bottom first, and luckily for me the boy with the very smallest prick in the room drew the desired prize. He was about fourteen, but such a pretty fair little fellow that I quite loved him at once.

His first action was to come and kiss me, then with one arm around my waist, stood belly to belly, and rubbed his much smaller prick against mine.

Just then one suggested that unless we blocked up the window the light would betray us, so as they wished to retain the candles in use, they took a couple of blankets off the beds, and put them up so as effectually to darken the windows.

The next thing was to make me lean over the bed on my face, so as to offer my bottom fairly to the attack of my young lover; they next took a little pomade from a pot, and put some both on my little hole as well as the head of his prick.

Being small there was not much difficulty about his getting in, and he soon began to afford me great pleasure, especially when, putting his arms round to my front, he began to frig my stiff member.

Looking round to see all that was going on, I found my lover also had one in his bottom, and the whole of them soon formed a perfect string in action, each one in the bottom in front of him, making a chain of eight links. There seemed quite a kind of electricity about it, as I fancied I felt all the pricks in my bottom by turns, and when at last it came to the spending crisis, one and all came together with cries of delight; whilst I also bedewed the hands of my partner with a few drops of spend, as I almost fainted from excessive emotion.

Of course other nights we changed places and partners, sometimes going in for a general suck all round and giving our bottoms a rest.

I got so fond of having a cock in my mouth that I could have eaten them, and at that time liked it better than anything.

I only stopped at that school a fortnight, for I was both fortunate and unfortunate at the same time.

My father was killed by accident, and mother had to take me home, because his affairs turned out so badly she could not afford to pay for my schooling; which, as it turned out, thus prevented my constitution being ruined for life by such early precocity; besides, it was all found out and the school broken up soon afterwards.

You may be sure these early impressions took a deep hold of my naturally warm disposition, although I had very few opportunities of again indulging. I knew it was wrong to do such things, and whenever

I did happen to get a young friend for a bedfellow, never failed to try on for a mutual frig.

I would lay beside a fresh companion till I fairly shivered with emotion, and would wait till he was asleep, or pretended to be so, my cock all the time as stiff as a bar of iron; then my hands would slyly and gradually slip under his nightshirt, and slowly work to the all attractive spot, gently try a few soft pressures till the cock began to respond to my caresses by a very perceptible swelling; then I got bolder, and generally my bedfellow would turn over and reciprocate my dalliances till we joined in a mutual fuck between each other's thighs, belly to belly. My favorite idea was to pull back the skin of my foreskin, and doing the same to my bedfellow's prick, bring the nose of his affair to mine, then draw the skin of mine over the heads of both cocks, and fuck each other gently so. What delicious thrills we had when spending, the seed seeming to shoot backwards and forwards from one to the other! Only those who have done it can at all realize such delicious sensations. Very seldom have I found a youth reject my caresses, although many of them would keep quite passive, and let me do everything.

Next day I could hardly ever look them in the face, but generally found them quite ready for another spree at night.

But so few chances occurred to me, and then only for a day or two at a time.

However, I met with an adventure with the other sex when I was nearly fourteen.

We had a young dairymaid about eighteen, a fine dark-eyed wench, very good looking, a strapping big, strong young woman, with rare plump arms and splendid full bosom, whilst as to her development of rump, to judge from the appearance outside her clothes, it was something superb.

My bedroom was in a garret at the top of the farmhouse, and a ricketty old staircase led up to my door, and then with a twist to the other side, without any landing, you could step up to Sarah's room (she was our only servant); so it was little more than a step across from my door to hers. At the bottom of our staircase there was a door which we could bolt inside, and so be secure from burglars or the other inmates of the house, unless they fairly broke in.

Of an afternoon, after she had done milking and all her work, Sarah used to go up to her room to wash and dress, and I noticed that even by daytime she bolted the staircase door. My curiosity was aroused, so slipping up to my room sometimes before her time for dressing, I used to take off my heavy shoes and watch her dressing through the keyhole of her door, but I never saw very much except those lovely titties and neck in the process of washing or changing her frock.

This went on for some days, and my elder brother being away at the time, I used to lay and think about Sarah for hours after going to bed; yet I dared not venture to do anything, and in fact was ignorant of almost everything about the opposite sex.

One afternoon, being rather more clumsy than usual, I stumbled against her door just as I was going to apply my eye to the keyhole, and not being fastened it flew wide open, exposing Miss Sarah in the very act of admiring her fine bosom in front of a small glass. How she blushed for a moment, but recovering herself at once, exclaimed: "Well I never, Master Jack. What do you think you will see now?"

I stammered out an excuse, but she asked me into her room, saying, with a laugh, "I know you thought you would see my legs or something, now, didn't you?"

"I know I did. You won't tell mother, will you, Sarah? I've often seen your beautiful big breasts, and wanted to see——"

"I never tell tales, Jack, if you don't. What did you want to see? Tell me," she said, with a most tantalising smile.

My assurance returned as I found she was not cross, so I told her that it was her fine bum that I so very much wished to see, adding that I would give a shilling to see it just for a moment, as I was sure it was a beauty.

"I don't want your money, dear," she replied; "but will you kiss it if I let you have a peep?"

"That I will," I eagerly replied. "Only let me lift your skirts, Sarah."

"And I must look at your's, Jack, and kiss it. Is it a bargain, dear?"

"I'll show as much as you do for a spree, so make haste," was my answer.

"What a nice little fellow you are. Give me a kiss first, and then we'll have a romp. Would you like to come and sleep in my bed at night, dear?" she asked, and I felt my breath almost sucked away, as she squeezed and hugged me to her heaving bosom.

You may be sure I liked nothing better, and assured her so.

As if by magic her skirts dropped down to her heels, and in a moment Sarah was dancing round the room with nothing on but her chemise, affording me exquisite glimpses of her splendid fat bum, and a soft brown muff which ornamented the lower part of her belly in front.

"Off with your things, Jack, before I'll let you kiss me, make haste, or your bum shall smart in the twinkling of an eye," she exclaimed, dancing up to me, her rosy face an animation and a devilment in her looks I had never seen before.

My face was burning. Her daring immodesty seemed to make me quite shamefaced, and I felt so abashed I hardly knew how to speak.

"How you blush, Jack; did you never see a girl before?" she asked, seeming to take pleasure in increasing my embarrassment. She kissed me again and again, as she almost tore my clothes off, till nothing but my shirt afforded the least protection against her ardent glances.

"Slip off that ugly rag, as I do," she exclaimed, letting her chemise drop, and thus abandoning the last slight protection to her nakedness. "I must hug you to my naked body, dear; it is so nice."

"Now kiss me, and I'll kiss you," she said in a soft, excitable voice, as she pushed me on to the bed. "Your little plaything is so stiff and beautiful, I mean to fondle it, while you kiss my bum!"

I resigned myself entirely to her directions, and laying on my back on the middle of the bed, she got over me face downwards, so that her open thighs just brought a hairy covered crack right over my face and almost blindfolded me as she pressed it down to my lips, which seemed instinctively to imprint kisses on what I had just previously been almost afraid to see.

Quicker than I can put it on paper, she had hold of my standing affair. At first she kissed my belly and thighs, laid her warm cheek by the side of my cock, then I felt her kissing its head, as her hands gently drew back my foreskin, and presently I could tell that it was well in her warm mouth, and being deliciously sucked, which made me repay her in the most ardent manner possible. My own tongue visited the lips of her crack, and I sucked and thrust it in as far as it would reach.

How she sucked at my pego, as she wriggled her crack over my lips, but it did not last long before she let down a regular flood of thick creamy spendings, which so excited me that I came also at once and shot my juvenile tribute into her mouth, as she greedily swallowed every drop.

"There, there," she said, almost with a sigh, "we've done it, Jack. It's so naughty; but isn't it nice, dear?"

Then she presently slowly raised herself off my body, and we lay for a short time side by side on the bed, kissing and toying with the most attractive charms of each other's person, till at last she jumped up and begged me to dress quickly for fear mamma should be calling for us.

"Take your things, and run into your own room, and be sure not even to look at me before anyone, or it will be sure to be noticed; and you know you can come and cuddle me again all night when they are all in bed."

As I sat at tea that afternoon I could scarcely eat or drink; nothing but the delights I had tasted with Sarah and anticipations of the coming night would run through my fevered brain, whilst my poor little cock every now and then stiffened again in my breeches, till I hardly knew how to restrain my feelings.

I tried to read a fairy tale, but it was useless, and at last my mamma, noticing how I kept flushing up, sent me off to bed about eight o'clock.

Ours was an early family, everyone generally getting to bed by ten o'clock; but how to pass those two long hours of expectation I was quite at a loss, as I lay tossing about on my bed with one hand gently frigging my awfully stiff affair.

However, I must have fallen asleep, as I well remember waking up in the dark and feeling someone in the bed, with her arms round me, and warm lips kissing my cheeks.

"It's only Sarah, Jack. I did not expect you would go to sleep and forget me so soon. Shall I go back to my own bed, dear?" she whispered in a low voice.

"No, no. Oh, pray don't, I love you so!" I whispered in return, as I began to repay her loving kisses.

"Let us both go into my room; the bed is more comfortable for two," she said, so we at once adjourned to her apartment and were soon comfortably cuddling one another again.

"Jack," she whispered "did you ever have any rude games with the boys at school?"

So I at once told her about my adventures, and how we used to put our cocks up each other's bottoms, etc.

I felt her actually tremble with suppressed excitement as she so nervously clasped me in her arms whilst I was telling her all about it.

"Don't you then know what a girl is like? I mean you didn't know till we kissed each other this afternoon, did you?" she asked.

"No; but I liked kissing you there, Sarah," I replied, as one of my hands indicated the spot. "May I do it again?"

"No; we'll play at mothers and fathers. You shall put your dear little prick in there. That's how babies are made by men and women, only we shan't do that," she said, as she very gently drew me upon her, and opened her legs and directed my pego to the gap of love, which was so longing to receive the little morsel.

I felt she was quite wet, and my affair glided into the well-lubricated aperture with the greatest of ease; but how deliciously warm it was! and I could feel the folds of her cunt close on my prick so delightfully that I at once began fucking as quickly as possible, glueing my lips to her's and pushing my tongue between her amorous lips, as she almost sucked my breath away. How she heaved up her bottom, and clasping her arms tightly round my slender body, kept me from being unseated by her restive steed.

"Oh! oh! oh, Jack! I'm coming, you darling—you duck of a boy, how you make me spend! Ah—r—r—r—re!" and she seemed almost to stiffen her body at the moment, whilst my cock, balls, and thighs were deluged by her thick creamy juice, which also trickled all down the crack of her bottom. Presently she recovered a little, and putting one hand down to my affair, withdrew it from her reeking cunt, and pointed it to the little hole just below, whispering as she did so, "Push in there, dear. Don't spend in my pussey, as even a boy like you might make me a baby if you come there; besides, I long to know what it is like. It must be nice, or the boys at school wouldn't do it."

"Oh! oh! it hurts though," she sighed, as I pushed on, and gradually progressed little by little; still it very evidently was anything but a painless operation, to judge from her sighs and suppressed murmurs. At last, however, I was chock-a-block, as the sailors say, and she gave me a kiss of satisfaction at having achieved our purpose.

"Now go on, Jack. It feels so nice, and excites me so."

At the same time her legs were thrown over my loins, and she heaved up her arse to every stroke of my living piston.

So tight, such a deliciously warm and throbbing sheath, delighted my little prick—I cannot describe how I felt; but it must have swollen up immensely. It felt ready to burst, and almost directly I felt the electric shootings which give such intense pleasure in the act of emission. My very soul seemed to melt into her vitals under these blissful sensations.

"How beautifully warm; how I feel it shoot up into me! Ah, this beats everything I ever felt before!" she sighed, kissing and hugging me in rapturous extasy.

"No, my love," I laughed. "You never felt it before when you have it in your bottom. I'm so pleased that you like our way, as I also like this little hole best."

She made me repeat the game without withdrawing, and all night long we were kissing and sucking each other's parts, till just as it was getting light we fell into a sound sleep in each other's arms.

After this first night we always slept together, but she would not always let me fuck her, as she told me too much of it might injure my health.

One morning she confided to me the secret that she often got a nice fuck in the cowhouse from our boy Joe, who assisted her in the milking. "And what do you think, Jack, I get him to do sometimes? Why, there is a long stool there which we put under one of the quietest cows that has beautiful long tits, then I lay myself on my back on the stool, and he puts one of the cow's tits right into my pussey and milks it right into me. It's beautiful, it's delicious, beats everything; no man is at all so good. It makes me come so when I feel the rush of the warm milk right up into my very womb. You shall see it, Jack, this very afternoon. I'll tell Joe you're all right, and we can have a good lark together, as your mamma is going on a visit somewhere this afternoon directly after dinner."

This was a chance for me. I had long wanted to get intimate with master Joe, who was a fine, plump, good-looking, ruddy-faced boy of seventeen, but he had always seemed so distant and shy, even to me his mistress's son; in fact it now seemed another instance of how "still waters run deep," as I thought how curious it was that he should be so free with Sarah.

As soon as my unsuspecting parent had started on her way, Sarah and I went to the cowhouse, where Joe met us with a smile of pleasure as we entered.

"Now, Joe," she said on entering, "let's get the work done as quickly as possible, and milk them all but Cowslip. Then you shall let Master Jack see how you milk her into me."

I had not long to wait, for there were only seven cows in all, and presently the long stool was placed under Cowslip, and Sarah stretched herself upon it, so as to bring her cunt just under the udder of the good-tempered creature, who seemed quite used to the trick, putting her nose to Sarah's face with quite an affectionate kind of kiss.

Joe quickly turned up her skirts till he quite exposed her belly up to the navel, then taking one of the cow's teats, he handled it a little, but not with a milking motion—it seemed to harden at once like a natural prick—and then inserting it into Sarah's cunt, he began the milking.

Her eyes seemed at once to sparkle with quite an unusual kind of brilliancy, as she exclaimed, "Go on, go on quick; it's beautiful!" heaving up her rump as if a man was fucking her, whilst it was most exciting to see the white milk spurting from her cunt at every fresh injection, running down the crack of her bottom and thighs, or hanging in pearly dewdrops about the silky brown moss which adorned her lovely mount.

My prick had been standing all the while I had been there, but this sight filled me with the most lustful desires, and I could also see by the protuberance of Joe's breeches that he also was in the same state, as his eyes were intently watching the operation of his hand, the twitching of her cunt, and every motion of lascivious girl.

I fairly shook with emotion, but with trembling hands I began to undo his breeches, and pulled them down to his knees.

Heavens! what a lovely prick stood before my starting eyes!

I nervously grasped it in my hand, and kneeling down printed hot and luscious kisses on its fiery head as I pulled back the foreskin. I could eat such a delicious morsel, and longed to swallow every drop of the pearly juice I knew my caresses would soon cause to spurt from his lovely cock. I took it fairly in my mouth, sucking quite ravenously, and rolling my tongue around it in the most wanton manner, whilst my hands were busy caressing a splendid pair of balls, contained in a tightly drawn up round purse, richly ornamented with almost black hair, which hung below the root of his white and bursting shaft.

Almost with a scream, he spent at once, as he shouted in extasy, "I'm coming; oh! oh!! oh-!!! you darling Jack," shoving his prick so fiercely into my mouth as almost to choke me as the hot juice spurted down my throat, to my infinite delight.

Presently he recovered a little, and changing the teats, went on milking into the delighted Sarah's cunt. She afterwards told me that the sight of Joe fucking me in my mouth seemed to double her pleasure.

Rising from my knees, I now let down my own trousers, and presented my own glowing prick to Joe's arsehole behind (for I was quite as tall as he was). He stooped a little so as to thrust out his bottom and facilitate my attack, so wetting my fingers in a pail of milk, I applied them to his fundament, moistening the head of my prick at the same time. He was evidently a maiden behind, and I had great difficulty in getting well in, but I had my arms round him, frigging his fine prick in front, and both were so excited that although I made him wince, as well as hurting myself, at last it was done.

"Ah! it's feeling nice now; push on, Master Jack. Fuck me well, frig away; I'm coming again. Oh! oh! I can't stop; do spend in me!" he cried.

Believe me, I did spend. I never had had such an emission before. It seemed to keep throbbing and shooting for ever so long and my prick grew both in size and length that day. It had never seemed so big and inflamed in any previous encounter with boys or Sally.

Whenever my mother was away we repeated these amusements, and I often also found chances of having Joe's tight arsehole on the sly, and he also obliged me the same way, but we never told Sarah for fear she should prove jealous. In fact now and then she expressed her suspicions of my love for Joe, as naturally it made me slightly remiss in my attentions to herself.

Soon after reaching the age of sixteen my mother succeeded in getting me placed at Messrs. Cygnet and Ego's, a large West End linendrapery house, which had a most aristocratic connection.

Here morals were very strictly looked after, and it was quite impossible for the youths to indulge in any sensual amusements in the dormitories.

In a few weeks my prick became so awfully troublesome for want of employment that I often had to retire to the closet to frig myself on the sly. The sight of the many handsome girls and young fellows had a perfectly maddening effect upon me, especially as they were all forbidden fruit, and I verily believe I should have ventured to risk it with some one, if chance had not favoured me with an adventure which afforded the necessary relief.

Early one afternoon, as I was busy behind the counter, I heard some one speaking to our principal shopwalker.

"Send a good variety of patterns, Mr. Gooser, let him bring them about four o'clock; my sister will then be at liberty to look them over."

Something seemed to strike me that I was indicated; so looking up I saw a very handsome young lady with an equally handsome man of about thirty, who was evidently her brother, speaking to the shopwalker.

"Certainly, my lord; he shall wait upon her ladyship without fail," I heard him say as he bowed them out of the shop.

Directly they were gone I received orders to go to Churton House, Piccadilly, the mansion of the Marquis of Churton, with quite a cab-load of rolls of silk for selection by the lovely lady, who I now found to be the Hon. Lady Diana Furbelow, his sister.

The portly flunkeys who ushered me up to her ladyship's boudoir were most obsequious in their attentions to me, and carried all my parcels up as well. In fact I was quite at a loss to account for such respect being shown to one who I knew in their hearts they merely regarded as a young counter-jumper.

"What is your name, sir?" said her ladyship, looking up from a book which she was reading as she reclined on an ottoman in a kind of loose dressing-gown, having evidently discarded her dress after her morning drive.

"Mr. Saul, at your ladyship's service, with a lot of silks for selection from Cygnet and Ego's. Will your ladyship be pleased to have them brought up?"

"Bring them up, James, and tell William I want some wine and biscuits, as I may keep this gentleman some time making the selection. When there are so many beautiful patterns it is so difficult to make up one's mind. Pray be seated, sir, for I'm sure they keep you on your legs long enough in those nigger-driving shops."

There was an indefinable something, besides the kindness of her manners, which at once put me at my ease with this beautiful lady, and my prick was so mannerless as to stand at once under the influence of her soft, loving eyes, eyes of an etherean blue, set under a lovely pair of dark eyebrows and ornamented with a fringe of dark lashes, through which she seemed to look at you.

There was just a slight perceptible flush on her pale cheeks, and to add to the charm of her exceeding beauty, she had a splendid chevelure of really golden hair, small pearly teeth, and cherry lips, which almost made me beside myself to contemplate.

"Help yourself to a glass of wine, Mr. Saul," she said. "You must need it; besides, I am so difficult to please, you will have no easy time of it in unrolling and rolling up again all those silks you have brought. No ceremony; help yourself."

"What; not pledge me?" she said, with an arch smile. "Pour me out a glass if you please, and hand the biscuits."

The blood rushed to my face, as I stammered out my excuse that I feared to take such a liberty.

"You will very likely have to come here pretty often, so pray make yourself quite at home. Here, I wish you every success in your business. Now, sir, drink, to me!" she said, raising the glass to her lips.

I did the same, wishing her ladyship every future happiness.

She pressed me to take a second glass, and then I proceeded to open out the rolls of silk for her inspection, and at the same time I felt a most extraordinary glow pervade my whole system, as if the wine had contained some very potent stimulant.

She seemed quite absorbed in the business of selection. Her pretty hands every now and then seemed to touch me quite inadvertently; yet there was quite a magnetic influence in them—such a thrill would shoot through my frame at the slightest contact.

Very few minutes had elapsed ere she appeared to become suddenly very faint, and sank back on the ottoman.

"Oh, sprinkle my temple with water, Mr. Saul. Don't call for assistance; it will soon pass off,"—as she saw me about to ring the bell. "Oh! oh! this dreadful cramp in my leg; it always comes when I feel faint. Do rub the right calf; chafe it as hard as you can," she cried out, in apparent great pain.

I sank on my knees by the side of the ottoman, and taking up her tiny right foot (I had never seen one so small before), chafed the calf as hard as I could.

I cannot describe how I felt at that moment, as my hands played over the smooth pink silk stocking which encased that delicate, but beautifully-moulded leg.

Looking up in her face, her head had sunk back on a cushion; the eyes were closed, but quite an expression of pain pervaded the lovely features.

She was insensible; what a chance! How could I resist pushing aside the slight coverings which so lightly veiled the seat of love. Heavens! she had no drawers on!

My hand stole up her lovely thigh, and was about to touch the spot itself, which I could see nestled in a little grove of auburn curls, between her closely-compressed thighs, when she seemed to awake with a sigh and a start.

"My God, what have you seen, Mr. Saul?" she said, drawing herself up and wrapping the dressing-gown closely round her.

My blood was in a boil, as I threw myself upon her, saying, in a deep husky kind of whisper, "My lovely lady, you have indeed permitted me to see too much of your charms to resist their ravishing influence. I must, I will have you, if I die for it!"

One of my legs was between hers, and I struggled to open them still more. She seemed to resist me with all her strength; we panted; we struggled; slowly but surely my superior strength seemed to prevail, the fiery head of my prick almost touched the lips of that delicious quim. I pressed my mouth to those pouting cherry lips of hers; I inhaled and sucked in luscious draughts of her fragrant breath.

Ah, ha, ha, she yields; her rigid limbs relax. I gain ground; the head of my prick enters between the throbbing lips of that heavenly cunt. I shove; I push on; it is in to the roots. Ye gods! what a paradise to enter; it seems like taking heaven by storm. The crisis seizes me, and a perfect torrent of my long-pent-up sperm floods the very bottom of her womb, and we both almost faint from excess of pleasure, and as I lay supine upon her I had the ineffable enjoyment of feeling the soft hugging pressure of those ivory arms, which now clasped me to her bosom, whilst her lips repaid my previous attention by a profusion of loving, billing kisses.

A chuckling laugh behind me recalled me to my senses, and turning round to see what it could be, to my horror I beheld the marquis himself standing frigging a very nice fine prick of his own, and evidently enjoying the sight of our conjunction.

"There's a lewd little bitch for you!" he exclaimed. "To think of my sister, the aristocratic Lady Diana, having a linendraper's assistant; but I'll punish you. You shall commit incest with me, your brother, and you, Mister Counter-jumper, shall look on."

His sudden appearance had in a moment reduced my cock to its normal state of limpness, and I withdrew quite abashed from the delicious cunt I had spent in.

"Slap my arse; bugger me; shove your prick into me as I fuck her, and you shall be well paid!" he almost shouted, throwing himself on his sister, and beginning to fuck fast and furiously.

"My pet, my love, my own Diana, no one shall ever marry you, you darling, although I must first be excited by seeing some beautiful boy have you. And you, sir, make haste to help me behind; it's the only way I can really enjoy my sister!"

Prick was ready again in less time than I can write it; the sight of a brother fucking his sister so excited me that I began to slap his bottom with my open palm as hard as I could with one hand, whilst the other was busy feeling his balls and handling the shaft of his fine stiff penis as it worked in and out of that lovely cunt.

"Fuck me! bugger me! or I can't spend!" he exclaimed, so nothing loth, I lubricated his fine hairy and wrinkled arsehole with spittle, and bringing the head of my cock to the tight-looking orifice I speedily effected an entrance.

What a fuck that was! He was evidently rather slow, although awfully excited, and both his sister and myself having just emitted a profusion of our essence of life, we were not so quick in reaching the spending point.

With both hands I frigged him, and tickled her clitoris, as he fucked away, whilst my prick was as lively as possible in his posterior aperture.

At last we came, and all three almost at the same moment; our bodies fairly quivering again and again as the electric thrills shot through our excited frames.

At last it was over, and both of them overwhelmed me with caresses till it was absolutely necessary for me to take my departure, when Lady Diana hastily selected several pieces of silk, whilst the marquis pressed a ten-pound note into my hand, and assured me I would very often have a chance of obliging both himself and sister again.

For a period of two years I continued to be their favourite, till, Lady Diana's health failing, the marquis took her to Naples.

It appeared, in explanation of this incident, that this brother and sister had always loved each other to excess since the age of puberty, and nothing would induce either of them to marry. Although the marquis at last became so blasé that he required the stimulating sight of seeing his sister fucked by a boy before he could enjoy her himself, she loved him as much as ever, and allowed herself to be used as a lure to seduce young fellows like myself, in order to pander to his depraved tastes.

I never saw the Marquis of Churton or his beautiful sister again, but a month or two afterwards I had to wait upon a rich city gentleman, the principal of a large financial house, who I shall call Mr. Ferdinand, a rather handsome but exceedingly blasé gentleman, between thirty-five and forty years of age.

Not to be too tedious with my story, I may say that I soon found out that his letch was to be frigged by a young fellow like myself, and many handsome presents did I receive from my generous patron for that and an occasional suck which I gave his prick sometimes by way of an extra treat.

Once he induced me to stop out all night, and the next day Mr. Gooser gave me my dismissal. It was done very kindly, but he assured me that the rules of Messrs. Cygnet and Ego's house could not be infringed by himself or any of the highest employés.

Mr. Ferdinand seemed rather pleased than otherwise at my misfortune, and promised to introduce me to a secret club, the members of which he assured me would only be too glad of my services at their pederastic seances, and my fortune would be at once assured.

This club was in a street out of Portland Place, and if you had looked in the London Directory you would simply have found it as the residence of a Mr. Inslip—a rather suggestive name, you will think, considering the practices of the members of his club.

I afterwards found that no gentleman was admitted to the freedom of this establishment unless he first paid an admission fee of one hundred guineas, besides a handsome annual subscription and liberal payments for refreshments and the procuration of boys, soldiers or youths like myself.

My financial friend duly introduced me to Mr. Inslip, who was soon very favourably impressed by my feminine appearance and well-furnished implements of love.

The very same evening there was to be a club meeting, at least a dozen gentlemen being expected to be present, so after having subscribed my name to a very fearful oath of secrecy, I took my leave of the proprietor with a promise to look in and be introduced to his patrons about 10 p. m.

Just as he was seeing me to the door there was a loud knock, and he opened it to a handsome, tall young fellow, with light auburn hair and deep blue eyes.

"The very man I want," said Mr. Inslip. "Let me introduce you to a new friend. Mr. Saul, Mr. Fred Jones. Now Fred, you know we have a soirée to-night. Will you take care of Mr. Saul till then, and bring him back with you? You can let him into our ways a bit by that time, and then he will be quite *au fait*."

"All right, guv'nor," responded Fred. "I like the look of him. So come along, my dear, and have a chop and cigars at my rooms," he said, turning to me.

Mr. Jones had been a soldier in the Foot Guards, and, bought out by Mr. Inslip as soon as the latter found what a useful youth he was, in great favour with the members of his club.

"We all do it," said Fred to me, as we sat smoking and sipping brandy and water after the chops he had invited me to partake of in his rooms. "It's the commonest thing possible in the Army. As soon as (or before) I had learned the goose-step, I had learned to be goosed, and enjoyed it, my dear; don't you, Jack?" he said, slapping my thigh and passing his hand over my most interesting member. "Now I'll tell you all about it. We'll keep ourselves fresh for to-night; but another day I mean to both fuck you and have you fuck me. Is that a bargain, my dear?"

Having assured him that I was perfectly agreable to be his wife or husband, whichever he preferred, at any time, he continued:—

"I was saying how common sodomy is in the Army. Our old major was the first to introduce me to it. He made me drunk, and next morning I found myself in his bed with him. Money was everything with me then. It always has been. Why, I used to be office lad to a solicitor at Liverpool, where I forged his cheque for a hundred pounds and ran away to London, had a damned spree for a week, lost or spent it all, then enlisted. It was the safest thing to do; the military rig-out so changes the appearance of a fellow.

"Well, I was speaking about our old major. Two or three quid squared me at once, and I let him get into my arse again, as no doubt he had done whilst I was drunk. That was the first time I really felt what it was like, and enjoyed it. My stars! how the old buck afterwards sucked my prick and frigged me till I hadn't a drop of spend left in me.

"In a very short time I got used to his ways, and used to abuse him, telling him what a beast he was, etc., which used to delight him, and he would give me an extra sov. for it.

"I have had lots of women, but do not care for them, for they do not make half so much of us as gentlemen do, although of course they always pay us. You can easily imagine it is not so agreable to spend half-an-hour with a housemaid, when one has been caressed all night by a nobleman.

"This is the experience of all the men of my regiment, and I know it is the same in the First, The Blues, and every regiment of Foot Guards.

"When a young fellow joins, someone of us breaks him in and teaches him the trick; but there is very little need of that, for it seems to come naturally to almost every young man, so few have escaped the demoralization of schools or crowded homes. We then have no difficulty in passing him onto some gentleman, who always, pays us liberally for getting a fresh young thing for him.

"Although of course we all do it for money, we also do it because we really like it, and if gentlemen gave us no money, I think we should do it all the same.

"Many of us were married; but that makes no difference. All we have to do is not to let the gentlemen know it, because married men are not in request.

"So far as I can see all the best gentlemen in London like running after soldiers, and I have letters from some of the very highest in the land. One gentleman, a nobleman, had me once in his own house, in the room next to his wife's boudoir. I heard her laughing, and talking, or playing on the piano, whilst her husband was on his knees before me, sucking my prick.

"We both laughed about it afterwards, especially when I asked him if he thought her ladyship would not like a dose from the same bottle?

"On one occasion five of us went with one gentlemen and acted with him or with one another for him to see, every kind of buggery, frigging and gamahuching. It was a luscious scene, just such as you will see to-night, my dear," he said, squeezing my stiff prick outside my trousers. "But wait till then; don't let my talk make you randy," he continued.

"That gentlemen was a clergyman, and one of the most liberal friends I ever had."

"Young fellows are quite as much after us as older men. I have often been fucked by young gentlemen of sixteen or seventeen, and at Windsor lots of the Eton boys come after us.

"I know two men in The Blues who are regularly kept by gentlemen, and one has an allowance of two hundred a year for allowing himself to be sucked.

"There are lots of houses in London for it. I will give you a list some day, where only soldiers are received, and where gentlemen can sleep with them. The best known is now closed. It was the tobacconist's shop next door to Albany Street Barraks, Regent's Park, and was kept by a Mrs. Truman. The old lady would receive orders from gentlemen, and then let us know. That is all over now, but there are still six houses in London that I know of. Inslip's Club, however, pays me best, so I am very little known elsewhere at present."

He never allowed the conversation to flag all the evening, and rattled on in the same style till nearly ten o'clock; and I think by the time we put on our hats to go to the club he had fairly told me all he knew, and considerably opened my eyes as to how the sin of Sodom was regularly practised in the Modern Babylon.

Mr. Inslip always opened the door himself, and at once ushered us into a small dressing-room, where we left our hats and other impedimenta, and under Fred's directions I assumed a charming female costume. He acted as lady's maid, fitted my bust with a pair of false bubbies, frizzed my hair with curling irons, and fixed me up by adding a profusion of false plaits behind.

Then he also dressed himself as a girl, and when we both looked in the glass preparatory to going to join the company, we appeared so pretty and feminine that I was quite in love with him, and clasped him to my breast as I imprinted hot burning kisses on his lips, whilst my hands groped under his clothes, and up his drawers, till I had hold of a splendid stiff prick. His eyes fairly shot fire as he returned my ardent kisses for a moment or two, and then suddenly wrenched himself away, with the observation that we must not make fools of ourselves. We could have plenty of that sort of thing some other time.

He had evidently heard Inslip's footstep, for that worthy appeared almost in a moment to ask how much longer we should be. He complimented us upon being two such pretty girls, and then said, "For this evening, Fred, your name is Isabel, and yours, Mr. Saul, is to be Eveline."

"Gentlemen", he said, as he ushered us into a fine large drawing-room, "these are the Misses Isabel end Eveline I had promised should be here to meet you this evening."

All rose as we entered; there were ten gentlemen and eight ladies waiting to receive us. It was a splendid apartment fitted up with mirrors all over the walls, whilst the windows were firmly closed and shuttered, besides the thick curtains which were drawn across them. Here and there were recesses filled by luxurious couches, before each of which stood a small table covered with the most exhilarating refreshments.

Two elderly gentlemen advanced and conducted us to seats.

Presently some one sat down to a piano and struck up a quadrille, and in a few moments we were going through the fascinating evolutions of a dance.

Our partners were particularly attentive to us, mine more especially so—in fact I can only speak for myself. He plied me with refreshments after every dance, and I could see was immensely taken with me. Now and then he would pinch my bottom, and after a little while slyly got one hand up my clothes and groped till he found my prick. His touch added fuel to the flames of lust by which I was already consumed; a very few touches sufficed to make me spend all over his hand, which I perceived gave him great pleasure.

About two o'clock in the morning the lights were suddenly turned out, and we were all in the dark.

"Now, love, I must have you," he whispered. "Every one has got a partner; and after I have fucked your delicious bottom, we separate and find another partner in the dark, so there can be no favouritism or neglect of any member."

He made me lean over the couch on my face, and lifting up my skirts behind he knelt down and kissed my bottom, buggering me with his tongue till the hole was well moistened; then getting up, I felt a fine prick brought up to the charge. It hurt me a little; but he was soon in, then passing his hands round my buttocks he frigged me most deliciously as he worked furiously in my bum.

How I thrust out my arse to meet every lunge! But it did not last long; we were both too hot, and came almost directly. It was a delightful bottom-fuck; but the rules precluded us from having a second, and we parted with a loving kiss, and went in search of other partners.

Before time was called about 6 a. m., I had had six different gentlemen, besides one of those dressed up as a girl. We sucked; we frigged and gamahuched, and generally finished off by the orthodox buggery in a tight arsehole.

I became a regular frequenter of Inslip's soirées, as I always got a fiver for the night, besides plenty of fun and refreshment; but contented myself with two nights a week, for fear of getting used up too soon, by which self-denial Eveline became a universal favourite.

The extent to which pederasty is carried on in London between gentlemen and young fellows is little dreamed of by the outside public. You remember the Boulton and Park case? Well; I was present at the ball given at Haxell's Hotel in the Strand. No doubt the proprietor was quite innocent of any idea of what our fun really was; but there were two or three dressing-rooms into which the company could retire at pleasure.

Boulton was superbly got up as a beautiful lady, and I observed Lord Arthur was very spooney upon her.

During the evening I noticed them slip away together, and made up my mind to try and get a peep at their little game, so followed them as quietly as possible, and saw them pass down a corridor to another apartment, not one of the dressing-rooms which I knew had been provided for the use of the party, but one which I suppose his lordship had secured for his own personal use.

I was close enough behind them to hear the key turned in the lock. Foiled thus for a moment, I turned the handle of the next door, which admitted me to an unoccupied room, and to my great delight a beam of bright light streamed from the keyhole of a door of communication between that and the one my birds had taken refuge in.

Quietly kneeling down I put my eye to the hole, and found I had a famous view of all that was going on in the next room. It put me in mind of the scene between two youths which Fanny Hill relates to have seen through a peephole at a roadside inn. I could both see and hear everything that was passing.

Lord Arthur and Boulton, whom he addressed as Laura, were standing before a large mirror. He had his arm round her waist, and every now and then drew Laura's lips to his for a long, luscious kiss. His inamorata was not idle, for I could see her unbuttoning his trousers, and soon she let out a beautiful specimen of the *arbor vitæ*, at least nine inches long and very thick. It was in glorious condition, with a great, glowing red head.

Laura at once knelt down and kissed this jewel of love, and would I believe have sucked him to a spend; but Lord Arthur was too impatient, as he raised his companion from her stooping posture, and passing his hands under Laura's clothes, as she gave a very pretty scream and pretended to be shocked at this rudeness, he turned everything up and tossed her on the bed.

As yet there was nothing to see but a beautiful pair of legs, lovely knickerbocker drawers, prettily trimmed with the finest lace, also pink silk stockings and the most fascinating little shoes with silver buckles. His lordship quickly opened Laura's thighs, and, putting his hand into her drawers, soon brought to light as manly a weapon as any lady could desire to see, and very different from the crinkum-crankum one usually expects to find when one throws up a lady's petticoats and proceeds to take liberties with her; but his lordship's love was only a man in woman's clothes, as everyone now knows it was Boulton's practice to make himself up as a lovely girl. There seems such a peculiar fascination to gentlemen in the idea of having a beautiful creature, such as an ordinary observer would take for a beautiful lady, to dance and flirt with, knowing all the while that his inamorata is a youth in disguise.

"What's this beautiful plaything, Laura darling? Are you an hermaphrodite, my love? Oh, I must kiss it; it's such a treasure! Will it spend like a man's love?"

I heard Lord Arthur say all this as he fondled and caressed Boulton's prick, passing his hand up and down the ivory-white shaft and kissing the dark, ruby-coloured head every time it was uncovered.

How excited I became at the sight you may be sure. I also longed to caress and enjoy both the fine pegos I had seen; but although my own prick was stiff almost to bursting, I determined not to frig myself, as I was sure of finding a nice partner when I returned to the ball-room. Still, I would rather have had Boulton than anyone. His make-up was so sweetly pretty that I longed to have him and him have me.

But to go on. I could see that the assumed Laura was greatly agitated. Her whole frame shook, whilst one of his lordship's hands seemed to be under Laura's bottom, and no doubt was postillioning her bottom-hole; and presently, seeing how agitated he had made her, he took that splendid prick fairly into his mouth and sucked away with all the ardour of a male gamahucher; his eyes almost emitted sparks as the crisis seemed to come, and he must have swallowed every drop of the creamy emission he had worked so hard to obtain.

His other hand frigged the shaft of Boulton's prick rapidly as he sucked its delicious head.

After a minute or two he wiped his mouth, and turned Laura round so as to present her bottom over the edge of the bed, then threw up all the skirts over her back, and opening the drawers behind he kissed each cheek of the lovely white bum, and tickled the little hole with his tongue, but he was too impatient to waste much time in kissing, so at once presented his prick to Boulton's fundament, as he held the two cheeks of his pretty arse open with his hands.

Although such a fine cock, it did not seem to have a very difficult task to get in, and he was so excited that he appeared to come at once; but keeping his place, he soon commenced a proper bottom fuck, which both of them gave signs of enjoying intensely, for I could fairly hear his belly flop against Boulton's buttocks at every home push, whilst each of them called the other by the most endearing terms, such as:

"Oh, Laura, Laura, what a darling you are! Tell me, love, that you love me! tell me it's a nice fuck!"

And then the other would exclaim:

"Push; push; fuck me; ram your darling prick in as fast as it will go! oh! oh! oh! quicker, quicker; do come now, dearest Arthur; my love, my pet! oh! oh!! oh!!!"

After seeing so much I slipped away from the keyhole, and went back to the company in the dancing room.

Park was there as a lady, dancing with a gentleman from the city, a very handsome Greek merchant, but I did not care for either of them, but sat for a while on a sofa by myself, watching the dancers and taking notice of all the little freedoms they so constantly exchanged with each other.

Presently Lord Arthur and Laura returned to the room and came and sat down by me, his lordship, to whom Mr. Inslip had previously introduced me, at once saying: "Allow me to introduce you two dears to one another Miss Laura, Miss Eveline. I must go away for a minute, and will be back directly."

Boulton seemed to take to me at once, and after a little ordinary conversation, whispered to me as he gave me a card:

"Come and see us in our rooms to-morrow, as we are. I know I shall love you; but there is no chance for it here. We must amuse our customers to-night."

This I agreed to, and soon after the lights were turned out and a general lark in the dark took place. I do not for a moment believe there was one real female in the room, for I groped ever so many of them, and always found a nice little cock under their petticoats, most of them quite slimy with spendings, they had been frigged so often.

At last it was over, but just as Mr. Inslip was going to hand me to his brougham, Boulton asked him to let me go home with them, and at once drove me off with Park to their rooms near Eaton Square.

END OF THE FIRST VOLUME

THE SINS OF THE CITIES OF THE PLAIN

Only 250 copies printed.

THE SINS

OF THE

CITIES OF THE PLAIN

OR THE

RECOLLECTIONS OF A MARY-ANN

WITH SHORT ESSAYS ON

SODOMY AND TRIBADISM

»—:o:—«

IN TWO VOLUMES

»—:o:—«

VOLUME II.

LONDON

PRIVATELY PRINTED

1881

JACK SAUL'S RECOLLECTIONS

*(**continued**)*.

—:o:—

SOME FROLICS WITH BOULTON AND PARK

As soon as we got to Boulton's place, he gave me a drop of his invigorating cordial, a lovely liqueur which seemed to warm my blood to the tips of my fingers; then we went to bed, and slept till about twelve o'clock, had breakfast, all dressed as ladies (I believe the people of the house thought that we were gay ladies).

Boulton assured me they hadn't a rag of male clothing in the place, all their manly attire being at some other place.

"I love to look like a girl, and to be thought one. I had such a lark the other day with a beautiful milliner at Richmond," he said, sipping his chocolate. "You must know I was stopping at the Star and Garter Hotel, and fancied a new dress; or, rather, I had seen this lovely milliner in her shop—she was the principal—so I went in, gave my order, requesting her to call on the Hon. Miss Murray at the hotel to try it on in two days' time.

"She was a lovely creature, nearly six feet high, but beautifully proportioned, with dark auburn hair, deep blue eyes, and such a lovely white skin, whilst her mouth was almost always on the smile, showing a lovely set of pearly teeth with which I was so much in love that I wanted to make her take my cock between her lips; besides, she was just slightly freckled, which is always a great charm in my idea.

"Miss Bruce, that was her name, called on me about twelve o'clock, as I was at breakfast, so I pressed her to take a cup of chocolate, and as I had expected her, she did not see the cordial at the bottom of the cup before I poured it out for her.

"Having elicited that she was not particularly busy, we sat chatting for some time about fashion and trimmings, etc., for I am as well up in all that as any lady in England.

"When I could see by the sparkle of her eyes that the cordial had considerably warmed her blood, I asked her to step into the bedroom to try on the dress.

"She was going to fit it on at once, and was about to remove my morning costume, when I exclaimed: 'Oh, not for a minute or two. I feel rather faint, my dear Miss Bruce. I must sit still a little. Do you mind giving me a drop of that cordial?' as I indicated a little liqueur case on the table. 'It will put me right at once. I often come over like that. Thank you. Now pray take a little yourself. It will do you good, and is so nice.'

"She followed my example, and seemed evidently to like the flavour of it.

"'Sit down, dear, by my side. There is no hurry about that troublesome costume.'

"Then as she sat down I gave her such a luscious kiss on her mouth, saying: 'You look so pretty; do excuse me, if you won't kiss me in return. I do so love to be kissed by nice people; not gentlemen, of course, but I am so fond of ladies if they will let me love them. Do kiss me, darling!' and I drew her face again towards mine and looked into those lovely deep blue eyes.

"She threw her arms round my neck as she blushed up to her temples, and said in a soft voice: 'How can I help it? You are so loving!'

"Then our lips joined in such a long-drawn kiss that I quite felt her heave with emotion. 'Do I excite you, darling, by such kissing?' I asked, and taking advantage of her confusion, I soon had one hand under her dress, and slipped it up to the seat of love. She scarcely resisted my advances at all.

"'You love, I must kiss it. For God's sake let me. I am so in love with you!' I said, slipping down on my knees in front of her, and before she could help herself my head was under her clothes and my tongue trying to tickle her clitoris, as my hands forced her yielding thighs apart. It was too much for her. The cordial had so warmed her blood she could hardly tell what she wanted; besides, I was a lady, and not a man, so there could be no harm in that, as she afterwards told me.

"How I did gamahuche her as she fell back on the sofa and let me have my way. She wriggled, heaved and sighed.

"I could hear her gasp out: 'You darling; you love! How nice; how delicious!'

"Then her spendings came in a thick creamy emission, and I sucked it all up, and delighted her so by the tittillations of my tongue that she soon came again.

"After a little I got up and sat by her side.

"'And you, love, won't you allow me to kiss and return you the exquisite pleasure you have just afforded me?' she asked, as she kissed me excitedly.

"I pretended to resist her attempts to get at my cunney, and at last blushingly told her that I was one of those unfortunate beings (which perhaps she had heard of) who had a malformation, something like the male instrument—in fact, it was capable of stiffening, and always did so under excitement, exactly as a man's would do.

"'But, darling,' I added, 'it is quite harmless, and can do no mischief like the real male affair. Now you, I know, will be too disgusted to want to kiss me, although I am dying for you to afford me that pleasure.'

"This avowal seemed to excite her still more, and she assured me that she had often heard of hermaphrodites, and that they could have women as well as a man.

"'And now, darling, I am more anxious than ever to see and caress the jewel you must have. I own I have often wanted to feel what a man is like, and you can oblige me without any risk if you will. Will you, my darling?'

"She had got to the object of her desires by the time she ceased speaking, and at once commenced to kiss and caress it; the idea that perhaps I might be a real man never seemed to occur to her mind.

"'Oh, do have me, Miss Murray. I should so like you to ravish me; my blood is on fire; I'm not in my right senses; the sight of such a darling fills me with such a longing that I can't restrain myself. If you don't do it for me, you shall never love my little fanny again!'

"She had it in her mouth directly and sucked it so lusciously that I felt I should spend in her mouth if I did not have her properly at once, so I jumped up and asked her to lie on her back on the sofa and open her legs well.

"She did so at once, and turning up both our dresses we were soon belly to belly; her hand kept hold of my prick and directed it to the mouth of her cunt herself.

"By heavens! she was a virgin, and so tight! but I clasped her round the waist, and pushed furiously; so much so that she fairly screamed with the pain and tried to shove me away; but the crisis came, I shot a warm flood of sperm into her tight sheath, which, besides easing it a little, so excited the dear girl that she heaved up her bottom to meet me, and as I happened to push hard at the same moment, John Thomas fairly crashed through all the defences of her unbroken hymen, leaving nothing but a bloody wreck behind, as he went in up to the hilt.

"She did not scream, but giving one long, deep-drawn sigh, fairly swooned away under me.

"I did not withdraw, but lay as lightly as possible on her, making my prick throb in the tight-fitting sheath which imprisoned it so deliciously. I could feel the folds of her cunt contract on my shaft of love with a most delightful spasmodic twitching, such as I had never enjoyed before, and in about five minutes she opened her eyes and, with a smile, whispered: 'Oh, dearest, what a dream! I dreamt I was smashed to atoms; then my soul soared away to heaven, and I have been in Paradise, tasting such exquisite sweets, such thrills of love, and now I wake up to find it is you, darling, and that dear thing of yours that gives me such pleasure. How I feel it deliciously filling every part of my womb! But you are not a man, are you, darling? you can't do me any harm, can you? Do tell me that, love, and I shall be happy; otherwise I should tear myself from your arms and burst into tears!'

"How beautiful she looked! such a lovely flush of excitement on her pretty face! how could I undeceive her, so I glued my lips to hers, as I murmured: 'No, darling; I'm not a man. I can't hurt my love!'

"'Then, darling, give me all the pleasure you are capable of with it,' she said, smiling and heaving up her buttocks at the same time as a challenge for me to go on.

"My God! what a fuck we had! She kept me in position till I had come four times. You would think my prick would have wrinkled up from exhaustion, instead of which I was so unnaturally excited that it swelled bigger than ever, and, although I did not spend again, we kept on ding-dong till I had fairly used her up and she had to beg I would let her go, as she had no more strength.

"How many times I made her spend it would be impossible to say.

"You won't be surprised to hear that that dress did not easily fit. She came so many times to try it on, and fucked me so dry, that at last I had fairly to run away from Richmond, and she will be very lucky if she does not get a big belly."

"Have you had many adventures of that kind?" I asked.

"Yes; plenty of them. I can tell you a lot of amusing adventures; but now, Eveline, Selina and I want a bit of fun with you, all alone by ourselves. It will be real love; not the mercenary, paid love we give our customers. I have got quite fond of you, and Selina won't be jealous. She will assist to make me happy; won't you, my darling?"

He rose from the breakfast-table, and opening the piano, ran his fingers over the keys; then motioning me to come to him, gave me a luscious kiss. "You darling Eveline, I'm sure your prick stands," he said, groping under my dress and finding it was as he said.

 "Now I will play you a nice piece, only I have a fancy to have you in me, and you must both fuck and frig me as I play to you," he said, as he made me sit on the music-stool, then raised my dress, and turning his bottom to me, lifted his own clothes and gradually sat down in my lap; as my stiff prick went up his bottom, my hands went round his waist, and I clasped that glorious cock of his, and he began to play and sing "Don't you remember sweet Alice, Ben Bolt?" from a parody in the *Pearl Magazine*, which he had set to music.

It had such an exciting effect on me that I shot my sperm at once, and I felt him spend all over my hands at the same time.

"Now, wasn't that nice, dear Eveline? Do you love your Laura a little bit?" he said, stopping and twisting his head round to give me a long sucking kiss on my mouth.

We kept our places, and he played several more pieces before we came again; then we adjourned to the bedroom, and he rang for the breakfast things to be cleared away.

The door was at once bolted, and then Laura asked me if I had ever been birched.

"Oh, yes," I replied; "and it's delicious when properly applied."

"Well then, Selina has not had any fun yet, and I don't think you will be any too ready to oblige her, so we intend to tie you up to the bedstead and see how soon the twigs will reinvigorate you, my darling. You know you were naughty and rude to me while I sat on your lap just now, so you must be punished for it at once."

It was useless for me to remonstrate against being tied up, as they were too strong for me, and I was soon secured by both wrists to the foot of the bed; then my skirts were pinned up and my drawers opened and let down to my knees.

"Ha, we have her now, the rude little slut!" exclaimed Laura. "Let me just pick out a proper little swishtail, and I'll take all that out of her naughty, impudent bum!"

I had never had a very severe birching, and rather dreaded they were going to be too hard on me. My poor prick had fairly shrunk up into his skin.

"Just look at that shrivelled-up thing, Selina. Did you ever see such a useless looking bit in your life? Stand clear and let me apply the reviver!"

Laura had got a long, thin bunch of birch, consisting of only three or four twigs, elegantly tied up with ribbons. Swish!—I heard it cut through the air, and if I had not been tied as I was I should fairly have jumped, such a stinging cut did I get.

"Ah! oh!! oh!!! Good God! not so hard, or you'll draw the blood!" I almost screamed out, as I winced under the pain.

"Ha! that was a beautifully practical illustration of how the birch should be applied. But perhaps you will like that better—and that—and that——?"

Three stinging cuts followed in rapid succession, and almost took my breath away.

It was no use calling out, so I fairly bit my lips to repress any cry of pain. It was not so much the weight of the blows but their smart, stinging severity. It soon made my bum all of a glow, and I began to experience a decided feeling of pleasure, my prick standing as hard as possible once more.

"Hold; hold; don't draw the blood, Laura dear!" cried Selina. "You've raised him finely. Now let me enjoy my turn; I long for him in my bottom at once. I can't wait while you play with him any longer; but you can touch him up when he is in me, to keep him to his work."

She was untying my wrists as she said this, and in less time than it takes to tell I was into her bottom and Laura's prick was in mine.

Never shall I forget the excess of lubricity of this triune fuck; we seemed all so excited; we fairly spent again and again, till nature was so exhausted that we lay in a confused heap on the bed, as our pricks soaked in each other's well-lubricated bumholes.

At last we thought we had had enough for one day and a night, so after taking a most loving farewell and promising to visit them often, I had a cab called and drove to my lodgings, where I can assure you I stopped two days to thoroughly rest and recruit my strength before venturing upon any further use of either bottom or prick.

Soon after this introduction to Boulton and Park, I had a funny adventure in the Temple. A note came from a barrister—in fact, a leading Q.C.—to say that Mr. Inslip had mentioned my name to him as likely to oblige him in a certain way, and would I be so good as to give him a call at his chambers at 4.30 p.m. next day.

Of course I went, and was shown into the private room of Mr. Horner, who I found had a lady with him.

He at once dismissed his clerk, with the observation "that he should not want him again to-day," and then, as soon as the door was closed, turning to me, said:—

"Mr. Saul, I am much obliged that you answered my note so promptly. It is not that I require your services myself, but this lady here wants a good fucking."

"Awful! the man's mad! Pray let me out!" almost screamed the lady in affright, as she made a rush to the door.

"Stop her! Don't be a fool, woman!" shouted Mr. Horner. "Didn't you come here to be fucked?—now just answer that question—yes or no—as we say in court. Tell Mr. Saul the truth."

The lady covered her blushing face with her handkerchief, and began to sob.

"Well I never; there's no understanding women at all. No wonder I never got married," exclaimed the Q.C. "Would you believe it? She came here to be fucked; I tell you the plain truth. I wanted a nice housekeeper, a free-and-easy one, that would humour me in anything I might fancy, and Miss Wilson here answered my advertisement. We were some time beating about the bush, till at last I plainly told her she would have to stand fucking, and must come to my chambers one afternoon on trial. She should have fifty pounds if I did not engage her, and two hundred a-year as lady-housekeeper if she pleased me. My God, I sent for you to fuck her. I didn't mean to do it myself; the fact is I require a very peculiar kind of excitement before I can get a cockstand. Now, Miss Wilson, you understand this is a nice young fellow, far nicer than myself, and I'm damn'd if I don't see him fuck you! We'll have a glass of fizz first, and then to business."

We had the champagne, then opening a door into another room I saw a bed. He gave me a sign, and I helped him to strip the frightened young lady.

She was powerless in our hands, and I noticed he took quite a particular pleasure in humiliating her and acting as rudely as possible in every way he could think of.

When she was stripped I commenced to throw off all my clothes, while he was amusing himself, kissing and tickling her cunt and clitoris till the poor young lady was almost dead with shame, besides being so excited that she could hardly contain herself.

"Now jump up," he exclaimed, "and don't spare the randy bitch. She's spent all over my fingers!"

Miss Wilson was too much overcome to attempt any resistance to my attack. She was not a virgin, so I soon got into possession of all she had and began to fire her blood still more by a good rapid fuck, Mr. Horner all the while slapping my arse with his heavy hand, as he laughed and almost screamed with delight.

This excited me immensely, so that you may be sure I did not spare our victim, especially as she was so beside herself with real erotic emotion that she heaved, wriggled, and squirmed about beneath me, and when the spending crisis came she was so carried away by her lubricity that her arms held me almost like a vice, and she actually made her teeth meet in the fleshy part of my shoulder.

Mr. Horner now joined in by putting one finger up my bottom, and then in a minute or two more I felt his prick take the place of his digit.

Mine was a most delightful position. I never enjoyed anything more than I did being sandwiched between him and Miss Wilson. Not one of the three seemed anxious to bring such a delightful conjunction to a close, and I am sure Mr. H. was all half-an-hour fucking my bottom, whilst I continued to make Miss W. respond in the most amorous manner possible to the motions of my excited pego.

She so far forgot herself as to say soft endearing things, and would every now and then ejaculate:—

"Ah! oh! how delicious! You make me come again; I can't help myself. I'm in heaven. Push, push now, there's a darling!"

Whilst the barrister was so carried away that he fairly screamed with delight.

I was handsomely rewarded for my services, and he took Miss Wilson for his housekeeper, and I afterwards often went through the same performance with them at his residence in Palace Gardens, Kensington.

The next adventure I can think of was at a garden party given in honour of the Prince of Wales; I will not say exactly where, but it was in the grounds of a noble mansion on the banks of the Thames, not a hundred miles from Richmond.

Lord Arthur took me with him, dressed as a midshipman, and I was presented to his Royal Highness as the Hon. Mr. Somebody, I can't exactly remember the name now.

After promenading for some time we met an elderly gentleman to whom he introduced me as a member of Inslip's Club.

"Eveline," whispered Lord Arthur, "this is Lord H——, who has heard of your attractions; let me introduce and leave you with him."

Lord H—— expressed the great pleasure he had in making my acquaintance, adding to Lord Arthur, "that he hoped his young friend was not too shy or mock modest."

Being reassured upon this point, he took me for a walk into some of the most shady parts of the grounds.

At last we came to a very retired arbour with a seat behind some rock-work and a small fountain playing in front.

"Just the spot for us," said his lordship. "Let me sit down here and make a better acquaintance, my dear!"

He was as loving as if I had been a young girl all at once, and then as I blushed at his observations about my appearance, and the promising bunch in the fork of my trousers, he proceeded to handle me, and pressed his lips to mine in a long breath-sucking kiss.

I wished he had been a nice young fellow, but his attentions soon aroused all my usually excitable feelings—my cock throbbed, and stood as stiffly as ever under the soft pressures of his hand, as he held it inside my trousers.

"I must kiss this darling jewel!" he exclaimed. "I love to swallow all the spendings of a nice young fellow like you, Eveline."

Then going on his knees before me, he put my prick in his mouth and sucked me most lusciously, whilst with one hand passed under my bottom he postillioned me in the most delightful manner possible, and when the crisis came in a few minutes he swallowed every drop with the greatest possible relish.

His next proceeding was to lower his breeches and get me to bugger him, which seemed to afford him equally exquisite pleasure, as his old prick stood as stiffly as possible. And after I had spent in his arsehole, he made me toss him off for a finish.

When we rejoined the company, one of the retinue of His Royal Highness begged for an introduction, and after some little conversation, assured me my fortune would be made if I would only consent to visit Berlin and Vienna, as he could introduce me to many of the highest personages in Germany.

Not caring to leave good old England, I politely declined his overtures, assuring him at the same time that I had not the least objection to be introduced to any of his eminent countrymen, should they happen to visit London.

On our return to town in the evening we found Boulton and Park waiting for us at his lordship's chambers. They wanted us to join in a special pederastic orgie, to take place the same night at the house of a certain young Earl, who had two young foreign pages just arrived, the one from France and the other from Italy, and their introduction into the mystic circle was to be the chief event of the night's programme.

Lord Arthur had another engagement, which prevented him coming with us, and so I went with them.

They had a private brougham in waiting, which took us to Grosvenor Square.

A very sedate and elderly footman ushered us upstairs to a dressing-room, which formed part of the Earl's own special apartments, a suite of six or seven rooms, rigorously set apart from the rest of the house, where none but his confidential servants and pages were ever allowed to enter.

At the time of our visit the Countess was out of town at Scarborough, assiduously carrying on an anything but innocent flirtation with a certain young Marquis; but the Earl, her husband, cared not a fig for that, so long as he enjoyed himself in his own way.

"His lordship will expect you in the billiard-room in half-an-hour. You will find your portmanteaus all right. They were placed here directly they arrived an hour or so ago," remarked the footman as he withdrew.

"Then we must not lose any time, my dear Eveline. You will find I have brought a charming costume for you," said Boulton.

Notwithstanding sundry loving jokes and liberties we were soon ready to see the Earl, and as we entered the billiard-room, found he had three other gentlemen with him, all young fellows like himself, under twenty-five or thereabouts.

"How are you, my dears? Laura and Selina, how lovable you both look; and this, I suppose, is the charming Eveline I heard so much of the other night at Inslip's. These are my regular chums, who call themselves Mr. Wirein, Mr. Cold Cream, and the Hon. Mr. Comeagain. You will, of course, find their names and pedigrees in Debrett if you care to look them up. Now, don't be bashful, and I will also introduce you to my three pages who are in special attendance on us to-night."

Saying which he opened the door of what looked like a large bookcase, and there stood three of the prettiest boys I had ever seen, each of them quite naked with his stiff prick in his hand.

The eldest, apparently, was a fair young French fellow about seventeen; the second an olive-tinted, but very handsome Italian boy of fourteen; and the third an exquisitely formed little [black] boy of about thirteen, with a prick that any man might have been proud of.

How I longed for the little black fellow!

The billiard-room opened into another fine apartment, used as a smoking-room, but in reality most luxuriously fitted up with most seductive-looking couches and ottomans, the heavily-curtained windows being separated by mirrors which extended from floor to ceiling.

His lordship conducted me to one of the sofas, whilst Laura and Selina took seats between the other three gentlemen.

Refreshments were served by the pages on little tables in front of us; then, at a sign from their master, they commenced a gambol at leap-frog all round the room.

This was a most exciting and beautiful sight—to see three such young Adonises flying over each other's backs, all their pricks as stiff as if carved out of stone; then what a study of graceful forms the ever-varying contour of their lovely figures presented to our fascinated gaze during the evolutions of their game.

In the midst of the game Lady Isabel was announced, and I at once recognized Mr. Fred

Jones, looking as beautiful as ever in his ladylike get-up.

This made four ladies and four gentlemen, besides the pages, and the Earl at once, handing me over to Mr. Wirein, sat himself down with Laura to a couple of pianos at the end of the room, and they struck up what I understood to be the "Slap-Bum Polka."

"Lay the boys across your laps, ladies, and slap them well!" exclaimed Mr. Cold Cream; so, catching hold of the little nigger beauty, I threw him across my knees, just as my partner got me on his lap, with my clothes raised and his stiff prick inserted between my thighs, one of his hands passed round under my clothes till he could get at my prick, and also frig that comfortably, whilst I turned up little Jumbo's bum and made him wriggle on my lap like a little eel at every smarting impact of my hand on his ebony posteriors.

The others were doing the same. Isabel was slapping Léon the French page, whilst Selina had Menotti the Italian, and right well did their hands bring the crimson flushes to the boys' bottoms as they slapped them as hard as they possibly could.

Our partners encouraged us by saying, "Bravo! lay on to them well. Make them spend under the slapping! Look how their pretty little pricks swell more and more at every blow!" etc., etc.

And so it was.

Then, just as we fancied our little victims really would spend their virgin essence, our partners shifted their cocks from between our thighs, and at the same time applying a little cold cream on the outside of our fundamental entrances, they slipped into our bottoms in the most delicious manner.

Mr. Wirein had a lovely prick, which just fitted me exactly, and to judge by the faces of Isabel and Selina they were equally well pleased with their partners' affairs.

Little Jumbo's eyes were fairly streaming with tears under the pain of my slaps. I was too excited to feel the least inclined to spare that ebony bum of his, for I scarcely knew what I was doing. His cock, quite seven inches long, young as he was, so took my fancy that I quickly raised him so that he stood on my lap and brought it right opposite to my longing lips, which instantly took the coal-black head into my mouth.

Did you ever see a nigger's penis when excited? The head of it is the blackest part of his body, and looks like a bit of black marble when the skin is drawn back. I wetted one of my fingers—the middle one of the left hand—and passing that arm round his bottom, kept him steady whilst at the same time I postillioned his little bottomhole; my right hand holding the shaft of his lovely prick or playing with his balls whilst I sucked his delicious jewel of love.

My partner was equally active. His prick swelled and throbbed in my bottom as I gently rose and fell upon it, whilst the hand that was frigging me kept well to its duty.

"You darling! you love! Oh, Eveline, I'm coming! Ah—ah—there it is, my love. Can you feel it shoot into you?" he exclaimed.

My own emission came at the same moment, and thoroughly lubricated his active hand as he afforded me the most intense pleasure in both parts at once; and to add to my emotion little Jumbo shot what I believe to have been his very first spendings into my mouth. My lips closed convulsively on the head of his pego, and with a long-drawn, continued suck, drained and swallowed every drop of his virility as it gushed into my longing mouth.

When I think of that conjunction even now my prick sticks up in a moment. Never before or since has my fancy been so excited or have I so enjoyed the very acme of bliss.

The others also enjoyed themselves immensely, and the Earl had Laura on his lap as he sat on the music-stool before the piano.

Selina now took Laura's place to play to us, and all being stripped quite naked, we made five very pretty couples. The Earl had Mr. Wirein; I secured Léon, the handsome French page; Laura the little Jumbo, etc., and we again commenced a most lascivious series of evolutions, forming our hands into arches in turns, under which the others would waltz, the leading couple forming the next arch, and so on and on round the apartment, pulling, squeezing, or slapping pricks all round, so as to keep them well alive and stiff.

When tired of this we retired with our partners to the sofas, and after refreshing ourselves with wines, jellies, etc., proceeded to have each other in the most fanciful ways we could imagine.

I made Léon lay over me the reverse way, so that I could take his fine pego in my mouth and postillion him with my fingers; all of which he was nothing loth to return with the greatest of ardour, till we both came in the other's mouth and racked off each other's spunk to the last drop. Then I made him turn round facing me as I still lay on my back, and so gradually bring his bottom down on my prick till I got it all in, and had him ride me a delicious St. George, as we kissed and tipped each other the velvet with our tongues, till we both spent again—I in his arse and he on my belly, his seed shooting along all over my breast.

This rather exhausted us for a time, but we lay in each other's arms, my prick still soaking and throbbing within the tight folds of his anus, and quite oblivious to all that was passing around us, when suddenly—whish! whish! whack! whack! came a birch on poor Léon's bum, and he would have fairly unshipped my affair from its delicious berth, had I not held him like a vice in my arms.

It was his lordship, the Earl, birch in hand, whilst the Hon. Mr. Comeagain was shoving into his bottom and frigging his prick for him.

He was called Mr. Comeagain (I afterwards found out) by his friends, as no amount of fucking ever seemed to take down the pride of his constantly standing member.

Another couple in similar conjunction were attacking with the birch the bottom of his lordship's lover, with others behind who passed their birching compliments from group to group, till young Léon's bum evidently received the quintessence of birch discipline. Heavens! how it made him move and dance on my delighted cock, whilst his affair, quite eight inches long, swelled and rubbed furiously on my belly as I lay under him.

This lasted a long time. The twigs fairly drew blood again and again, but added immensely to our enjoyment; whilst the Earl seemed to take the greatest possible delight in letting many of his strokes sting the tenderest parts of my inner thighs, and even my prick itself, if it happened to be exposed so that his rod could touch it up.

We screamed, laughed, and actually shed tears now and then, till at last it ended in the usual voluptuous emissions, which drove us almost beyond our reason from the excessive pleasure of the supreme moment.

This is only a trifle of what we went through before daylight put a stop to the further development of pederastic ideas for that time at least. All I know is that it took a good week's rest to make me feel fit to pay my next visit to Inslip's Club.

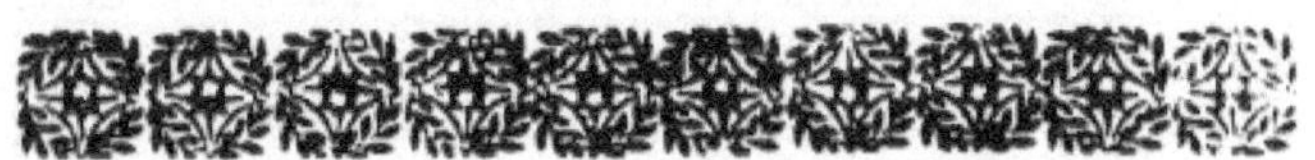

FURTHER RECOLLECTIONS
AND INCIDENTS

Only lately I have been introduced to two curious members of the Mary-Ann profession.

The first is known as Young Wilson, who is a very handsome youth of sixteen or thereabouts. He is about five feet two or three inches; very fair and pretty; with chestnut hair, dark blue eyes, and a set of pearly teeth which, combined with the rosy colour of his cheeks, makes him an almost irresistible bait to old gentlemen—or for that to young ones too—who are addicted to the pederastic vice.

We are very much in each other's confidence, so he let me into the secrets of his way of doing business.

One afternoon, as we were smoking and drinking champagne together, he suddenly commenced:—

"Do you think, Jack, I ever let those old fellows have me? No fear, I know a game worth two of that. You see, I never bring them home with me, and in fact always affect the innocent—don't know where to go to; am living with my father and mother at Greenwich or some out-of-the-way part of London, and only came to the West-End to look about and see the shops and swells, etc. If a gentleman is very pressing I never consent to anything unless he asks me to accompany him to his house or chambers. Once got home with him, I say, 'Now, sir, what present are you going to make me?'

"'Stop a bit, my boy, till we see how you please me,' or something very like that is the answer I generally get.

"'No; I'll have it now, or I'll raise the house, you old sod. Do you think I'm a greenhorn? I want a fiver. Don't I know too well that little boys only get five or ten shillings after it's all over? But that won't do for me, so shell out at once, or I'll raise the house, and a pretty scandal it will be!'

"That frightens them at once, so I almost always get at least five pounds, and sometimes more, as I take care to write and borrow as much as I can afterwards. There's nothing like bleeding one of these old fellows; and young ones are better still—they are so easily frightened."

He told me lots of tales of different people he had victimized in that way.

My other acquaintance, George Brown, comes on a different line of business. His plan is to pick up a swell, and ride about with him in a cab.

Many gentlemen are too nervous to take a boy home with them, or, in fact, to go to any house; but they like to get a young fellow in a cab, and either frig him or get him to do it to themselves.

G. B. would do all this, and wait till his prize was quite or nearly drunk; then rob him of his pocketbook, purse, or watch, as the case might be, very frequently even taking the rings off his fingers if he had any.

"Jack," he said to me the other day, "what a fool you are not to go in for the same lay as I do. You would get hundreds where you now only get tens.

"I had a rare lark with a Jew the other day. I knew he belonged to some City financial firm. He was too fly to get drunk; but took me down to the Star and Garter at Richmond on a Saturday afternoon (no doubt he had been to his synagogue in the morning). Well, we had a first-rate dinner, and by way of dessert I handled and sucked his rather worn-out prick till he spent, and he did the same to me; but I don't like Jews—they are so dark-complexioned, and both taste and smell rather strong—so I made up my mind to make him pay well for it.

"At length when he ordered a last bottle of fizz, and took out his purse to pay the bill, I could see he had very little more than a tenner left, which no doubt was intended for me; and so it was. Directly the waiter was gone out of the room, he tossed it across the table to me, saying: 'There's a little bit of paper for you, George. It's good pay for an hour or two, my boy. I wish I could make money as easily!'

"Of course I pocketed the flimsy; but never made any remark, except: 'Is that all for what I have let you do?'

"'Why, you don't even thank me for being liberal!' he remarked rather angrily.

"'Nothing to thank you for: I could wipe my arse on that! I mean to have a cool hundred; as I know it's nothing to you, who can swindle more than that any day in the City. Shall I call at your Cornhill office for it on Monday, or will you give me an I.O.U.?'

"'You bugger! You shan't have a damn'd penny more!' he growled out, putting on his hat. 'I'm going!'

"'Not till you square me, Mr. Simeon Moses!' I said, speaking as loudly as possible. 'You know you have been acting indecently towards me, and showing me a volume of the "Romance of Lust!" Would you like a bobby to find that book on you?'

"You should have seen him start as I mentioned his real name.

"'Hush! hush! for God's sake speak a little lower! What do you want? I'll send you the money.'

"'No you won't! I'll call for it anywhere you like to leave a hundred quid for me; but you must give me the rings off your fingers as security, to be returned when I get the money, on my word of honour.'

"He was too frightened not to comply at once, and told me to take them to a certain house in a little street out of Harley Street, any time after ten o'clock the next Sunday evening.

"I knew the house very well. It was kept by a great big bully, who had been a soldier, so, thinking perhaps there would be a little trouble in making him hand over the tin, I borrowed a small life-preserver from a friend by way of precaution, then went for a settlement.

"The bully opened the door himself.

"'Has Mr. Simeon Moses left a hundred pounds for me?' I asked.

"'Your name's George Brown, I think. Step into the parlour, and I'll see you presently,' he growled.

"Half-an-hour passed, and he still kept me waiting, so I gave a furious ring at the bell, which brought him in swearing at me for my damn'd impudence.

"'Now, Bill Johnson—you see, I know your name, and what's more, I know the games you carry on here—no humbug!' (bringing out the life-preserver and striking the table so as to make a regular mark in the mahogany). 'Have you got the money or not? I shan't stop, and Mr. Moses may whistle for his rings if I don't get it now!' I said, speaking loudly.

"'Damn it! yes. Only don't make a row. But he told me only to give you ten pounds and keep the rest!'

"'Give me ninety and keep the ten. I don't mind a fair commission,' I replied, and so we settled it at once, and had a good laugh over the sodding fools, as I stood a bottle of fizz."

After telling me the foregoing tale, he went on:—

"Did you ever hear that I was four years in the Reformatory at Red Hill? That was where I first had a prick up my arse."

"No," I replied. "But do you mean to say such things can be done there?"

"Yes," said George; "and if it had not been such a hell of a place I should have been a good scholar. Of course, the boys are supposed to go to school and work in the grounds. As for work, it was nearly all play; and none of us cared for the good-natured old schoolmaster, and so never learnt much.

"As to the sleeping arrangements, I was in what they called a dormitory—it ought to have been called a back-door-mitory. There were over twenty of us boys and lads in the one large room.

"As soon as we were locked in for the night, one of the biggest of them, observing me for the first time, says: 'Hullo! here's a greenhorn. We'll soon make a free-man of him!'

"They crowded round me, just as I had almost got my clothes off ready to get into bed with another of about my own size (I was fifteen).

"'What's your name?' 'How long are you sent for?' 'Have you ever had a cock up your arse?' etc., etc., was asked by one and the other of them, and they soon found out that in the latter respect I was quite innocent.

"In a trice I was thrown upon the bed, and held down on my back whilst all of them spat on my prick to make me a free-man; so, knowing it was useless to resist, I took it all as good tempered as possible, and hoped it would soon be over. But I was soon undeceived, for they proceeded to spread-eagle me on the bed, face downwards, by tying my wrists and ankles to the four corners of the bedstead; then a couple of pillows were pushed under my belly, so as to raise my bottom up a little. Then the biggest boy got up behind me and put his stiff prick to my arsehole.

"'Ah! oh! oh!! you hurt. I won't stand that. I'll tell the master in the morning!' I screamed out, and then began to cry.

"In an instant they tied a handkerchief over my mouth, whilst someone got hold of my prick, all greasy and slimy as it was from the spitting, and began to frig me, whilst the one behind me was trying to get his tool in.

"He pushed and pushed. It was impossible for me to scream, yet it was like forcing a bar of iron up my bottom. The pricking and stretching sensation was awful, and I do believe I should have been greatly injured if he hadn't spent his juice, and so eased the passage a bit. This enabled him to get right in, and I could feel his prick swelling and palpitating inside my bottom, whilst I felt so stretched and tight that I was really afraid for him to move.

"However, the feeling of distension went off after a bit, and it began to feel far nicer, especially after a few gentle moves on his part; then presently he spent again, and it felt so lovely and warm and nice, as it shot up into me; so much so that I began to wriggle about under the curious and pleasurable sensations he had aroused within me. My blood was on fire, and tingled in my veins to the tips of my toes and my finger ends, whilst their delicious frigging made me spend all over the pillow under my belly.

"The captain of the room having thus opened up my virginity, as they called it, had to withdraw; then one after the other got into me, and spent so quickly that it oozed from my bum and ran down the cheeks of my bottom, over my balls, etc. I was perfectly inundated with the slimy mess, but enjoyed it immensely; such a succession of stiff pricks revelling in my arse excited me so that I came again and again, as they continued to frig me; till at last the gag was removed from my mouth, and I was asked if I would tell the governor now, and as soon as I answered, 'No,' they let me loose.

"All night long the boys kept the game up, either fucking each other or sucking one another's pricks, and I can assure you I thought it was a beautiful game, which quite reconciled me to the confinement.

"Sometimes a new boy would be obstinate; then he was sure to be treated with the greatest possible cruelty. They would tie him down as they did me, and then flog his buttocks with a pair of braces with the buckles on till his rump was as raw as a beefsteak.

"It would take days to tell you of all the sprees we had at Red Hill.

"There was one young fellow, who, being rather of a superior education to the rest, was made a junior teacher in the school. Well, do you know the boys of his class would actually frig him as he sat at his desk to hear their lessons, for the head schoolmaster was mostly asleep, and no one else dared say a word. This fairly broke his health down, and he had to go into the infirmary.

"What games there used to be in the kitchen! The head cook was a great, strong woman of about forty, and had another woman almost like herself as assistant, and they were allowed half-a-dozen boys to help them. They were not always the same boys, but every morning the head cook would select those she liked, and march them off to the kitchen, so as, she said, to give every one a turn—and a good turn it was. We had to fuck both the women. They would each of them do the whole half-dozen, and fairly fuck us dry, and I have seen the boys throw them down and slap their fat arses till they screamed for mercy; then we would bugger them and frig them till they almost fainted from exhaustion.

"I don't mean to say that this was done every day, but perhaps once or twice a week, when they knew the governor was gone out. He used to come round first, and then as soon as he was gone the spree was started."

A few days ago George Brown, when a little under the influence of Bacchus, let me partially into another secret of his, which affords a partial clue to how so many unaccountable mysterious disappearances are always being mentioned in the papers.

"Do you know, Jack," he said, "what I do when things are a bit slack? I can always earn a poney (twenty-five pounds) if I take a little girl of about fifteen to a certain house in Paris; in fact, they will give me an extra fiver for every year she is under that age, so that a girl between eleven and twelve is worth forty pounds and all expenses paid. Now and then I get them a boy for a change, as they are in great demand for the rich visitors to Paris, especially for the Americans, who are nearly all sodomites. You heard of the case of General Ney, who shot himself the other day? Well, he was a regular customer to a certain Mme. R—— that I know, but they were too greedy, she and her ponce; always wanting money, and threatening the General to tell his wife and mother-in-law if he didn't shell out, so at last the poor fellow blew his brains out. If the boys or girls turn out obstinate, they are outraged with brutal violence, and then disappear no one knows how, but I have nothing to do with that.

"A fortnight ago I went down Whitechapel way, and dropped on to such a nice, pretty boy. He was a shoeblack, and, although only about thirteen years of age, beautifully formed and well hung with fine light golden hair, blue eyes and cherry lips. I fell in love with him myself. Whilst he was blacking my boots I asked a lot of questions about what he earned, etc., and soon found that he lived in a refuge, where they kept nearly all he brought in every night to pay for his schooling and board, etc., as he had no parents or relatives of any kind.

"Here was a chance for G. B., so I soon got him to promise to meet me near Moses' shop in Aldgate in the evening, and the result was I bought him a rig-out as a page, had his ragged-school livery made up into a parcel and sent back to the refuge, and took him off in triumph to my lodgings, a fresh place I engaged for that purpose that very afternoon. He was my page, and had a little bed made up in an anteroom next my own bedroom.

"I had four rooms en suite at three guineas a week in a nice street in Camden Town.

"Next day I bought him some more clothes, shirts, hose, etc., and had him well bathed; in fact, he made a handsome little gentleman when dressed in mufti.

"He seemed delighted at the change in his prospects, and the jolly blow-out of good things at every meal; so in the evening, after supper, I asked him how he would like to go back to the Ragged School Refuge again, as I did not think I should keep him very long.

"You should have seen the tears come into his beautiful eyes, as he threw himself on his knees and begged I would keep him, that he would die for me, and do anything he could to please me.

"It was some time before I would appear at all moved by his appeal; then I said: 'Well, Joe, will you promise never, never, to let out any of my secrets or what games I may play with you? Now swear it, sir, on the Bible!'

"So I made him take a fearful oath, which I felt sure had a great effect on him after his Sunday School teaching.

"'Bring me that small bottle of liqueur off the sideboard, Joe,' I said, as soon as he had taken the oath. I had a little of it in some water myself, and gave him some. You know, Jack, the stuff it is, and what an exciting effect it has upon everyone.

"'Now I want to examine your figure,' I said, 'because I won't keep a boy unless he is well formed everywhere; so just strip yourself, my lad.'

"I should not have thought he had so much sense of decency; but he blushed as scarlet as the most delicately bred youth could have done, and the sight perfectly delighted me, as it was a proof of his being a real virgin as yet.

"However, he did not hesitate, although the wavy blushes kept flushing across his pretty face as he threw aside his clothes, and presently stood quite naked before me, whilst the liqueur had such an effect that his fine little cock, quite six inches long, was as stiff as a ramrod, and evidently caused him considerable embarrassment.

"'Come to me, Joe. You look all right; but I must feel you all over, to see if you have any blemishes. How's this?' I exclaimed, touching his prick with my hand. 'Is it always sticking up like that? Put your hand into my trousers. You won't find me so. It's awfully rude, sir!'

"He was afraid of displeasing me, or I should never have got him to unbutton my trousers and put his hand on my prick; but he did, and pulled it out to view, as I ordered him to do. It was limp, but I knew his touch would have the magic effect very soon.

"'There, sir,' I said, 'why are you different to me? See if you can make me the same. Take the head in your mouth, and draw back the skin.'

"I could see he did not like it, but did it to please me. The touch of his warm lips and the soft pressure of his hand brought me up in a moment. It quite filled his small mouth; but I placed my hands on his head, and ordering him to suck it, and tickle it with his tongue, kept him to his task till the crisis came, and I almost choked the pretty fellow with my spendings.

"'Ah, oh, delightful! It's heavenly, Joe. If you please me like that I'll never part with you, my dear boy!' I exclaimed, carried away by my feelings. 'Here; kiss me, my dear boy!' as I raised him on my lap, and glued my lips to his, sucking my own spendings out of his mouth. 'It was so awfully delicious, Jack!'

"'Did that give you such pleasure, sir?' he asked in a kind of whisper.

"'Yes, Joe, my darling. I'll make you feel the same for yourself presently,' was my reply. 'You shall sleep with me, and we will now go to bed as soon as I am undressed. Take your clothes into your own room, and come back to me naked, just as you are.'

"We both got on to my bed in a state of beauty unadorned, and I sucked his little cock till I felt sure he must come soon, then, kneeling up on all fours, I ordered him to shove it into my bottom. He was too excited not to be ready to do anything I told him at once, and besides, there was no difficulty about his getting into me, as I could take a much bigger affair than his. Still, my fancy was awfully excited at the idea of having his virginity, and to think that his maiden spend would be in my arse.

"The little fellow came quite naturally to the business, and fucked me so beautifully that I spent in his hands as they clasped round my body and held my prick as I had directed him to do; then presently his shoves became more rapid and eager, and I felt his warm sperm shoot right up into me in a delicious jet of love juice, as he almost fainted on my back from the excess of emotion it caused him.

"'Oh! oh! what is it? How funny, how nice to feel so!' he ejaculated, between laughing and sighing. 'Oh! I suppose that it's the same kind of pleasure that you felt when I sucked you.'

"'Now, Joe,' I replied, 'you know what it is like, you will let me do it to you. Isn't it beautiful?'

"He kissed me, and told me I might do anything I liked with him, he loved me so; only he feared my big affair could never be got into his small bottom, and I could see he was rather afraid of the attempt. But I soon reassured him, and got him to kneel up for me as I had done for him; then, anointing the delicious looking pink hole with some cold cream, I brought Mr. Pego to the charge. At first I could make no impression; but having got my finger in, and opened up the way a little, I succeeded in getting a slight lodgment, which made him scream with pain and apprehension, especially when I began to push on a little further.

"'Ah! oh! dear sir! Oh! oh! pray don't; you'll split me! Oh! oh!' etc.

"Being afraid his cries would be heard, I reached a pocket handkerchief, and before he knew what I was about, had him effectually gagged.

"It was managed without losing my place, then with one hand putting a little more of the cold cream on the shaft of my prick, I gave a tremendous shove, and got a little further in. It must have been awfully painful, for he writhed and struggled to free himself from me, and went flat on the bed with a deep sigh, which would have been a scream but for the gag.

"The fact that I was inflicting awful pain only added to my lust, and regardless of consequences I pushed on till his virgin bottom had been completely ravished, and I could see little drops of blood ooze from him at every motion of my prick, which was also stained with blood, sperm, etc.

"I had spent; but the idea was so exciting that I kept on till I had done it three times, and the tight aperture became quite easy, and I felt the gag might be removed with safety.

"From what I could see of his face he was both crying and laughing in an hysterical state, so I thought I had better stop for that night at least, and it was a long time before I could bring him round to perfect sensibility.

"I had him again the next night, but it was awfully painful to poor Joe; then I took him to Paris and sold him for a hundred pounds—he was so handsome I wouldn't take less.

"Did you ever hear there is a small and very select club in Paris, where they practise every kind of cruelty, and even sometimes kill their victims. That's where, I believe, the refractory victims are finished off, but I don't know much for certain."

There are many more like young Wilson and George Brown, who have particular specialities for turning the pederastic vice to account, but I will now go on with my own experiences:—

Not long ago I had a rather mysterious note, asking me to call upon a gentleman at his chambers in

Brook Street, Grosvenor Square. I soon found out that he was a young nobleman of great wealth, so made up my mind to wait upon him.

He went by the name of Mr. Carton, and received me so graciously, and without the least ostentation, so that I was perfectly at ease with him from the very first moment.

"I heard of you, Mr. Saul, from a friend of mine who is a member of a certain club you visit. They call you Eveline, do they not?" he remarked, as soon as I had taken a seat.

Receiving my affirmative reply, he went on: "Then we perfectly understand each other. I require your assistance in a little delicate business, which I would not mention had I not been very well assured of your discretion. Of course, you know, I shall pay handsomely. The fact is I come of a very curious family. Both my father and mother (whom I need not mention) had most peculiarly erotic fancies, so I suppose that it is born in us. I am the youngest—not yet attained my majority—and have two sisters, one twenty-two and the other twenty-three years of age, and as beautiful as they are amiable, yet as lustful devils as angels can by any possibility be. The eldest seduced me, her brother, before I was sixteen, and soon let her sister into the secret.

"They are too wise to be fucked in the regular way. (God only knows how they came to know so much, but I suspect our French master, as he taught me a thing or two besides my lessons.)

"Well, as soon as they had made me their own, I had to bugger them, or let them gamahuche me, whilst I did the same to them. It has gone on for a long time.

They are both considerable heiresses, and determined never to marry and lose their liberty, but they find me quite insufficient to keep pace with their lustful ideas, so I want you to give me your assistance.

"We have got the most beautiful dildoes possible to be obtained in Paris, with which they fuck my bottom, whilst I do the same to either Emma or Eliza, as the case may be; but we are all of opinion that the real living instrument is so much to be preferred. By the bye, did you ever fit on a dildoe just above your own prick, and fuck a girl with it in her cunt, whilst at the same time you bugger her bum-hole with your pego? That is what I often do for them, and I think it must be awfully delicious, to judge from the state of excitement it throws them into; and besides, I myself, by stretching the imagination a little, fancy it is a real man's prick which I can feel rubbing against mine, with only the thin membrane (almost as fine as a French letter, which you know is the sole division between the two holes), between the two pricks. It's so delicious!

"You make up as a beautiful girl, and let them find out your male furniture as the game developes itself, and let the direction of affairs take its chance. They have a fancy for indulging in a little flagellation this evening if I can procure them a subject. They have read so much about it in books, especially in the "Birchen Bouquet," that they think it will add materially to their lustful appetites if they can flay a girl's bum by way of a prelude. You will catch it smartly, but the guerdon shall be equal to the pain. Are you agreeable? If so, go home and dress; then be here about 10 p.m. You will be shown up at once. Take the name of Miss Eveline Birch if you like."

He gave me a fifty-pound note, and said he hoped I would be punctual to the time named, which I assured him I would be.

I had enjoyed the thrilling effects of the rod too well when administered by Boulton at his apartments, so I now readily agreed to Mr. Carton's proposal, who, when I returned at the appointed time, I found with two beautiful young ladies.

"Allow me to introduce you, Miss Birch," he said, placing a chair for me, "to my two sisters, Lady Emma and Lady Eliza Carton. My dears, this is Miss Eveline Birch, the naughty girl who has come to be punished. Her papa and mamma have given me carte blanche to whip her till she confesses her liaison with a young officer in the Guards and promises never to speak to him again. Won't it be fun, dears? But not for her. I rather guess it will be a serious business for her delicate etceteras; you understand what I mean."

"Then don't give her time to think about it," said Lady Emma, as she and her sister rose in a very stately manner from their seats. "We are going into the next room, and shall be ready for her in two or three minutes. You had better give her a glass of wine to keep up her spirits."

I had hardly time to swallow a second glass, as Mr. Carton said they meant real business and would be back in a jiffey, before they threw open the door and reappeared, each of them having discarded her dress. They had only on their white petticoats, set off by handsome corsets, which displayed all the glories of their splendid bosoms to the best effect; and when I add that they were both lovely brunettes, with blue-black hair, dark hazel eyes set under splendidly arched dark eyebrows; long, drooping eyelashes; cheeks like a mixture of milk and roses; and the whole set off by ruby lips and pearly teeth, you may imagine it was a sight to move St. Anthony himself, especially if he could have caught a glimpse as I did of fine knickerbocker drawers, trimmed with costly lace, and lovely legs and feet in white silk stockings and Parisian boots, high-heeled and sparkling with diamond buckles.

Each had a lovely swishtail of birch in her right hand; not heavy rods, but just four or five pliant twigs of considerable length, elegantly tied together with blue velvet and magenta ribbons.

Advancing to me, "Come, Miss Eveline," said Lady Emma, "allow us to conduct you to punishment. We have a nice ladder in the next room, and our brother here shall enjoy the sight of your humiliation and disgrace."

"You shan't whip me! I didn't know what I was sent here for. No; indeed I won't, ladies! touch me if you dare!" I exclaimed. "Let me go! I've had enough of such nonsense!"

"Here, Walter, help us," they appealed to their brother. "She shall soon change her tune, the impudent hussey! What a joke to think she didn't expect it!"

Mr. Carton, who had placed himself before the door to prevent my attempted retreat, threw off his coat, and then all three seized and dragged me, in spite of my pretended resistance, as I cried and screamed by turns. Their excitement seemed to give them extraordinary strength, and I was soon fastened up by my hands to the ladder, and my dress, all in tatters from the struggle, was at once pinned up round my waist, then my drawers were opened behind, just as I found one ankle tied by some kind of cord to the bottom of the ladder.

"That's right, Eliza," cried Lady Emma. "Leave the other foot loose. Now the wicked girl shall get her deserts—my arm shall ache before I give over whipping her! What a horribly fast girl she must be to flirt and go on with officers of the Guards! How do you like that, Miss Eveline? and that? and that?" giving my poor bum three terribly sharp cuts.

I bit my lips to restrain any cries.

"Ha, you don't speak. Just let the naughty girl's drawers down to her knees, will you, Eliza dear?"

"Why, she's a man!" almost screamed Lady Eliza, when the drawers were let loose. "Look, sister! look! Don't spare the horrid creature!"

They both blushed deeply, especially when they saw that their brother had prepared a surprise, and was rather enjoying their confusion.

Lady Emma muttered something about "Dirty wretch, I'll pay him out!" and then, suddenly recovering herself, rained a perfect shower of cuts on my poor rump, whilst Lady Eliza, also seemingly in a great rage, took up another rod and helped her sister to cut me up.

How I screamed, and fairly yelled for mercy. "Oh, for heaven's sake, do, do forgive me, ladies! Your brother made me do it, and now sits there laughing at me! I beg your pardon. Oh! oh! oh! indeed I do!"

Mr. Carton was almost beside himself with excitement, and had got out his prick to frig himself. It was a beautiful specimen, about eight inches long, with a fine ruby head.

Their blows never relaxed; the small tips of the twigs cut round my buttocks till I was fairly excoriated and bleeding all over from the small of my back to the middle of my thighs, and the blood trickled down my legs, whilst neither prick nor balls escaped their merciless attack. Still, it was not so awful as one would imagine. The pain soon became dulled, and then was succeeded by a beautiful glow; such a lovely sensation—it is almost impossible to describe—pervaded my whole frame, and they must have seen it indicated in my face, for, throwing aside their rods, they let me loose, and embraced me with tears in their eyes.

Mr. Carton threw off all his clothes, and tore off the petticoats and every rag of covering from his two beautiful sisters.

Lady Emma was my mark at once, for she threw herself over a bed, projecting out her rump, which I considered an invitation to me to attack her lovely bottom. My cock was in such a furious state of lust and so distended, but I never gave that a thought.

How she winced as she first felt the hot head charging the tight little brown hole! but putting one hand behind her with a little cold cream on one finger, she greased the end of Mr. Pego; then, taking him in hand herself, directed my engine of love to the wrinkled entrance.

How bravely she met my attack; but it was soon effectual, and I glided into Paradise—such a warm, tight, juicy sheath throbbed upon and held my delighted prick! I was going to enjoy the sense of possession for a few moments, but was startled by a smart attack on my own sore bum; the cheeks were pulled apart, and I felt the head of Mr. Carton's affair battering for admission; then one hand was passed round to my front, where it groped to feel how I was getting on in his lovely sister.

This made me look round, and I then saw that Lady Eliza had fitted on a dildoe, and was just ready to get into her brother's bottom. What a luscious scene that was; and how lovely the two aristocratic young ladies looked!

He was into me in less time than I can write it, and the exciting effects of the previous flagellation made me almost beside myself. Each shove I gave into the bottom of the lovely Lady Emma I had a corresponding one from her handsome brother, who was pushed on to do his best by Lady Eliza behind.

A very few of these thrilling motions brought us all to a crisis. I felt his warm sperm shooting up to my very soul, just as my own spendings did the same for his sister, and we kept the same position till we all came together again.

After this luscious bout the two sisters sucked our pricks till we were as stiff as ever, then each of us fitted on a dildoe, and had them so in both holes at once, but I had the Lady Eliza for a change. Giving full scope to my imagination in this conjunction, I fully realized all the delights of which Mr. Carton had spoken at my first interview with him. It was indeed delicious to feel, as it were, two pricks rubbing against each other inside the dear girl, with only the thin membrane between them.

After this we made the two sisters lean forward and present their posteriors over the edge of the bed; then we made both of them feel a little of the realities of birching, till they fairly cried for mercy, and begged us once more to let them have our dear pricks in their bottoms.

That is how we passed the first night, and ever since I have been quite a favourite with them and their brother.

THE SAME OLD STORY

»—:O:—«

ARSES PREFERRED TO CUNTS

»—:O:—«

Since Nero had his mother, and Caligula fucked his horse, I believe that incest, sodomy, and bestiality have been fashionable vices.

I know one man, a Q.C., who regularly keeps a goat, which he prefers to either man or woman.

Another, a young nobleman of twenty, acts the part of Œdipus, and is passionately in love with, and fucks his own mother. Still, no doubt sodomy bears away the palm over all other vices.

I know a recent case in which a widow, keeping a small shop near Leicester Square, had a lodger who occupied her first floor for the last three years. Recently one evening after shutting up, she fancied she heard a noise in the front passage, but could see nothing, so as the man who usually put up the shutters for her had not gone, she asked him to wait a little while in the kitchen and listen. After about half-an-hour he fancied that he heard shuffling and whispering in the passage, so taking off his boots, he crept softly upstairs, and suddenly striking a match, saw Mr. Parsons, the first floor lodger, in the very act of getting into the bottom of a soldier, who had his breeches down and at once bolted out of the door without waiting to put himself in decent order. The lodger slunk upstairs, and took his leave next day.

Just as this is going to press there is a case in the London *Daily Telegraph* of July 9, 1881, in which a corporal of the Scots Guards is caught in the act of committing an unnatural offence at a coffee house in Lower Sloane Street. He gets committed for trial, whilst his companion, who has the luck to be Secretary to the German Embassy in London, is claimed to be dealt with by the German Government, and sent home to Vaterland, which is no doubt all that will happen to him.

The prevalence of sodomy amongst schoolboys is little suspected of being so general as it really is. Only lately a medical man of large practice was called in to consult with the master of a large academy, where it appears the scholars had learnt something much more interesting than Latin or Greek. His tale is given just as he related it to the doctor.

"A day or two ago, sir, my suspicions were aroused as to something highly improper going on in the sleeping rooms at night, so I determined to find out all the facts by ocular demonstration. Having several vacancies in the school, there happened to be a small room of three beds quite empty.

"This I availed myself of, and on Wednesday afternoon, when all were out in the cricket-field, I made some peepholes, so that they gave me a full view into two rooms on either side.

"The little room was supposed to be locked up, and also the master (myself) was thought not to be at home; so I slipped upstairs a couple of hours before bedtime, and locked myself in.

"By-and-bye they all came laughing upstairs, accompanied by two young ushers, one of whom slept in each room to keep order.

"By standing on the beds I had a full view of everything going on.

"'Now, Mr. Smith, let's see if your prick is sore after having three of us last night!' I heard one of the biggest boys say, and looking into the room, there was a rare romp going on. Four boys had thrown Smith on a bed, and were trying to unbutton his trousers, and at last got out his cock—it was a good size, and stiff as possible. I then saw Charley Johnson, a boy of fifteen, take it in his mouth and suck it, whilst another boy did the same with his pego, and so on till everyone but the usher had a prick in his mouth.

"I was too spellbound by the sight to make a noise or interfere. The fact is, doctor, I couldn't help frigging myself; and we all seemed to come at the same time.

"After this they began to quietly undress, so I took a peep into the other room, and there, by God, sir, the boys were fucking each other's arses! It drove me nearly wild. If I don't stop it they will draw me into their practices, and I can't resist the temptation my peepholes afford; so what is to be done I don't know. Besides, my school would be ruined if it were found out."

The doctor advised the schoolmaster to have everyone, ushers as well as pupils, medically examined one by one, and then he (the doctor), would pretend to find out from appearances all they had been doing, and try to frighten them out of doing it again by describing all the awful effects of pederasty.

Wouldn't many of our readers have liked the doctor's job?

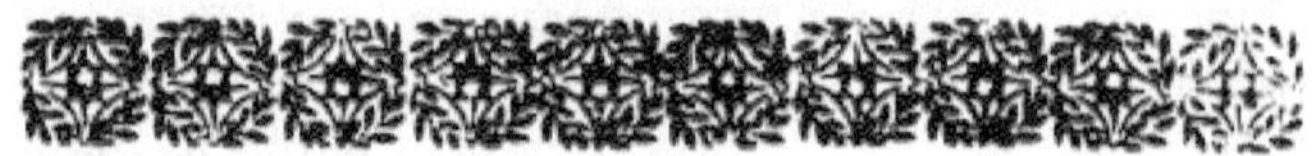

A SHORT ESSAY ON SODOMY, ETC.

Sodomy appears to have been one of the most important of the Roman vices and amusements; it was not by any means considered improper. We are speaking of sodomy with males, for we do not find anything much said about sodomy with women in the literature of the Roman day.

We say now a woman is all cunt, and the Marquis de Sade says that he must be a beginner indeed who has not had a boy, or made a boy his mistress. Martial treats sodomy with women good naturedly, and no doubt the Romans practised it. Many moderns are given to having women in the bottom, and most men who have gone in for anything like dissipation have done it now and then, and we sometimes hear of marriages being made unhappy from that unfortunate taste in the husband; but we think that with modern Europeans (except in Turkey, Greece, and part of Italy) it is quite the exception to find a man wedded to that practice; but with the ancient Romans it must have been a vice too common to be even alluded to.

If women are all cunt now what must they have been then?

Sodomy with males, with the above exceptions, is still rarer in the present day, and although we have made the most careful research, we do not know of many professional male sodomites in London; and when we were boys we remember a gentleman who kept a tall young fellow, a Creole, near Leicester Square. Our criminal reports show that such things do take place, and it is not long since that I was in court and heard a gipsy found guilty, first of all of having his own donkey, and afterwards a neighbour's little boy.

The offence is common in France.

Ambrose Tardieu speaks of having investigated two hundred and seventeen cases of passive sodomy—not always cases of French subjects—and speaks of the extraordinary enlargement of the *sphincter ani* arising therefrom. The vice is evidently attractive, from the number of things different admirers of it have inserted in their anus, in default of something better, such as knitting-needles, bottles and glasses; and he especially speaks of bottles of Hungary waters and eau de Cologne being inserted in the bottom-hole, also pieces of wood, and he mentions that in the latter case the whole fist of the surgeon could be introduced into the anus.

Another person, for a bet, put a tumbler up his bottom; and two children, the brother five years old and the sister seven, were caught one day putting spoons, carrots, and potatoes up each other's bottoms; and he mentions that the anus of the little girl was so dilated that it was nearly confounded with her vagina.

These facts give us some idea of the enlargement of the anus that may arise from sodomy, and help to explain some of Martial's epigrams.

There have also been some interesting remarks privately published by a recent traveller through the realms of the King of Bokhara.

He speaks of that monarch having two wings to his harem, one for boys and one for girls. When the King would have connexion with one of his boys, the latter is well purged and brought to the King fasting, scents and oil being injected up his bottom. Then the boy has his dinner to give him courage and spirits to amuse the King, after which his Majesty has the boy in the presence generally of two or three of the royal wives. This traveller speaks of the salacious ways of these boys, the enlargement of their bottom-holes, and growths around the orifice, which made it appear very like the private parts of a woman.

Tardieu speaks of this growth too, but he also speaks of other developments, as well as the consequences of passive sodomy, such as piles and various disagreeable matters. We think, too, that the King of Bokhara's habit of purging his boys before having connexion with them corroborates Tardieu's statement and the observations of many others, that the effect of being continually buggered (and Tardieu suggests as well the use of laxative ointments), is to so relax the *sphincter ani* that it will not retain the faeces.

In the most civilized places of the present day sodomy with males is rarely practised—with females it is practised oftener; but in Rome it was the habit, the recognized habit, and it only became hateful when the man always received the attention and never gave. In those days men loved a lusty fellow as much as women do now, and the lusty fellow could give as much pleasure to a man as he could to a woman, and be thought none the worse for it.

The vice was so general and fashionable that the chastest of the Cæsars, Augustus, was charged by many mouths with practising it; but Suetonius says, excepting his weakness for deflowering little girls, all the charges brought against him were calumnies.

Tiberius revelled in sodomy, and was surrounded by lusty Catamites, and rendered his name imperishable by indelibly connecting it with the Spintriæ. At this chaste court Vitellus was apprenticed, and soon acquired the name of

Spintria, raising his family by his prostitution, and showing when he in his time came to the throne, what a long train of evil one bad man in power can lay.

Caligula's mutual prostitutions with his pantomimic friend were well known, as was also his connexion with certain hostages; and the state of Roman decency may be presumed when we are told that V. Catullus, a young man of consular family, bawled out publicly that he had been having the Emperor until his back ached.

Cladius stuck to women, although he saw no harm in boys being debauched. Even his own son-in-law (to show the prevalence of the vice), we may observe, was stabbed and murdered while in the act of having his favourite boy.

Nero, of course, is not behindhand, and shows himself a true Roman Emperor by having the young Aulus Plautius by force, and then having him executed—the terrible result of worn-out desires, the irresistible impulse to remove from the face of the earth the man or woman you have satiated yourself with.

Our old friend Vitellus, when he came to the throne, managed the state entirely by the advice of the lowest classes, at the head of whom was the freedman Asiaticus, and his cabinet council was nothing but a series of mutual and unnatural pollutions.

Leaving Titus and the Eunuch, and Catamites, we will say one word on Galba, who bears the palm of Roman sodomites. He had no taste for women, nor had many a better man. He liked males, which was nothing uncommon; but he only fancied them when they were past their prime, and there he stood alone in his sodomy—he had not even the excuse of saying that the plump hips and smooth face of the boy resembled a girl. As another celebrated piece of royalty was fond of bad oysters, his taste was for old men—for men who had lived too long to enjoy pleasure or to give pleasure to anyone. But Galba, even when old Icelas brought the news of Nero's death, as he was sitting surrounded by friends, rose, kissed the old gentleman, and requesting him to make "a clear coast," led him into a private room, and had him. We can only say it would have been much more like Galba, if he had had the old gentlemen there and then before all the company.

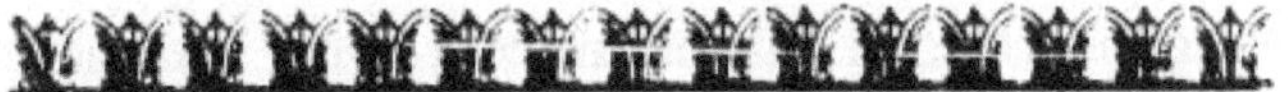

TRIBADISM

Dogging the heels of sodomy walks tribadism, a vice which every man in his heart looks on with kindly eyes. This sister vice appears to have existed from all ages. It is at least as old as sodomy, and still lives, aye, flourishes amongst the supposed modest maidens of our day. In all civilized Europe it exists among single women who have been debarred from men, generally in a narrowed sense, rarely taking other form than mutual frigging. But amongst some prostitutes of the upper class, and a few matrons of educated vicious tastes, it flourishes, the Frenchwomen bearing the palm. In the latter case gamahuching comes into free play; one woman loves another as jealously as ever a man could, and we have known instances in England of great unhappiness ensuing from one tribade giving up her inamorata for another man or woman; and in one memorable instance the forlorn one taking a revenge that very nearly involved the ruin of both.

The Count de Grammont mentions an instance in his memoirs of Miss Hobart, a maid of honour at the court of Charles the Second, being forbidden the royal presence for endeavouring to violate another maid of honour.

It is not clear how she was doing it, and it certainly is a mystery why that debauched monarch should have been so severe upon her.

No one can read Juvenal without being convinced that in Martial's time tribadism flourished in Rome. His descriptions of the feasts of the Bona Dea leave no doubt of it.

If he did leave any doubt Martial clears it up by the pointedness of some of his epigrams. It flourished even to women with enlarged clitorises (hermaphrodites) having boys.

This is perfectly rational. Sodomy and tribadism go hand in hand. Where one reigns the other flourishes, and in their development they are nearly identical vices. Boys debarred from women frig themselves, frig each other, and then have each other, and are fortunate if they do not grow up to be sodomites. Girls debarred from men do the same with their own sex, and bloom into perfect tribades by a gamahuche.

This is one end of the stick; the other is as when a man, having plunged into all the possible debauchery with females, at last resorts to sodomy, or where a woman, say a prostitute of good position with many friends, gets satiated and tired when she has exhausted every letch of the male fancy; then she turns to her own sex for a new and piquant pleasure.

It is not long since we were sitting in a café in the Haymarket when a Frenchwoman of about thirty walked across the room to a young English girl and offered her ten shillings to be allowed to kiss her cunt.

THE END

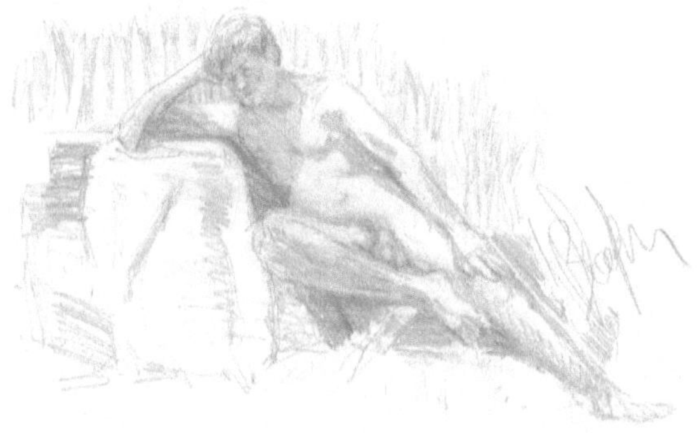

Figure 1 Pencil sketch of young man by James Bleeker used with permission.

9 798224 052301